DANIEL & ESTHER

Israel in Exile

John MacArthur

THOMAS NELSON

Since 1798

MacArthur Bible Studies

Daniel & Esther: Israel in Exile

Published in Nashville, Tennessee, by Nelson Books, an imprint of Thomas Nelson. Nelson Books and Thomas Nelson are registered trademarks of HarperCollins Christian Publishing, Inc.

Originally published in association with the literary agency of Wolgemuth & Associates, Inc. Original layout, design, and writing assistance by Gregory C. Benoit Publishing, Old Mystic, CT.

"Unleashing God's Truth, One Verse at a Time®" is a trademark of Grace to You. All rights reserved.

Thomas Nelson titles may be purchased in bulk for educational, business, fundraising, or sales promotional use. For information, please e-mail SpecialMarkets@ThomasNelson.com.

Scripture quotations are taken from *The New King James Version.* © 1982 by Thomas Nelson. Used by permission. All rights reserved.

Some material from the Introduction, "Keys to the Text" and "Exploring the Meaning" sections taken from *The MacArthur Bible Commentary,* John MacArthur, Copyright © 2005 Thomas Nelson Publishers.

ISBN 978-07180-3-4788

First Printing April 2016 / Printed in the United States of America

HB 04.29.2024

CONTENTS

INTRODUCTION

In 605 BC, the Babylonians defeated the army of Egypt at the Battle of Carchemish and became the strongest nation in the ancient Near East. Due to this victory, all of Egypt's vassals, including the small kingdom of Judah, became vassals of Babylon. The Babylonians followed up this great victory at Carchemish by invading the land of Judah that same year. After conquering the nation, they began to carry some of the nation's ruling elite into captivity in Babylon.

Among the young men who were taken was a man named Daniel, who, along with three close friends, found himself serving in the courts of the Babylonian King Nebuchadnezzar. Daniel rose to prominence in Babylon and lived a long life faithfully serving a succession of kings in two different empires. Years later, around 486 BC, a king named Ahasuerus (also known as Xerxes) came to power in Persia, and he took for his wife a young Jewish woman named Esther.

While the experiences of these two Jews were very different, they both faced dangerous situations that threatened their lives because of their faith in God. They held fast to their beliefs, put their complete trust in the Lord, and witnessed His mighty hand at work not only in their lives but also in the lives of their people. In this way, both Daniel and Esther learned the vital lesson that God is sovereign and faithful to those who call on His name.

In these twelve studies, we will examine the lives of these remarkable individuals and witness the bold actions they took in the face of daunting circumstances. We will see how both Daniel and Esther made the critical choice of standing up for God and the people of Israel even when their lives were at stake. We will also look at some of the insidious characters who sought to destroy them and follow the rise and fall of empires and kings in the region.

Through it all, we will learn some precious truths about the character of God, and we will see His great faithfulness in keeping His promises. We will learn, in short, what it means to follow God wholeheartedly and walk by faith in him.

THE BOOK OF DANIEL

The book of Daniel bridges the entire seventy years of the Babylonian captivity from 605 BC to 536 BC. In nine of the twelve chapters, the prophet provides revelation from God through various dreams and visions. Daniel was God's mouthpiece to the Gentile and Jewish world who declared God's present and future plans.

AUTHOR AND DATE

Several verses in the book identify the writer as Daniel, whose name means "God is my Judge." Daniel was taken captive from his noble family in Judah, deported to Babylon, and assimilated into Babylonian culture for the task of assisting with the imported Jews. There he quickly rose to the role of statesman by royal appointment and served as a confidante of kings, as well as a prophet, in two world empires.

Daniel spent the remainder of his long life (eighty-five years or more) in that city, living beyond the time he described in Daniel 10:1 (c. 536 BC). It seems most probable that he wrote the book shortly after this date but before c. 530 BC. Daniel 2:4–7:28, which prophetically describes the course of Gentile world history, was originally (and appropriately) written in Aramaic, the contemporary language of international business. Ezekiel, Habakkuk, Jeremiah, and Zephaniah were Daniel's prophetic contemporaries.

BACKGROUND AND SETTING

The idolatry of the northern kingdom of Israel led to its downfall in 722 BC to the Assyrian Empire. When Assyrian power ebbed by 625 BC, the Neo-Babylonians conquered Assyria (along with its capital, Nineveh) in 612 BC, Egypt in the following years, and Judah in 605 BC. The long-continued sin of Judah, without national repentance, led to this judgment from God, for which Jeremiah, Habakkuk, and Zephaniah had given warning. Earlier, Isaiah and other faithful prophets of God had also sounded the alarm.

Daniel was among one of the first groups of deportees taken to Babylon in 605 BC. After he was transported there, the victors conquered Jerusalem in two additional stages (597 BC and 586 BC). In both takeovers, they deported more Jewish captives (Ezekiel was deported during the second takeover in 597 BC). The book thus begins in 605 BC with the exile of Daniel and his three friends, continues to the eventual demise of Babylonian supremacy in 539 BC (when the Medo-Persians conquered Babylon), and goes beyond to 536 BC.

HISTORICAL AND THEOLOGICAL THEMES

Daniel was written to encourage the exiled Jews by revealing God's program for them, both during and after the time of Gentile power in the world. Prominent above every other theme in the book is God's sovereign control over the affairs of all rulers and nations and their final replacement with the true King. God had not suffered defeat in allowing Judah's fall but was working His sure purposes toward an eventual, full revelation of His King, the exalted Christ.

A key aspect within the main theme of God's kingly control is the Messiah's future coming in glory to rule the world over all people. He is like a "stone" in Daniel 2 and like a "son of man" in Daniel 7. In addition, He is the Anointed One (Messiah) in 9:26. Daniel 9 provides the chronological framework from Daniel's time to Christ's kingdom.

A second theme is the display of God's sovereign power through miracles. Daniel's era is one of six in the Bible with a major focus on miracles by which God accomplished His purposes. God, who has everlasting dominion and the ability to work according to His will, is capable of miracles, all of which would be lesser displays of power than was exhibited when He acted as Creator in Genesis 1:1.

Daniel chronicles the God-enabled recounting and interpreting of dreams that the Lord used to reveal His will. Other miracles include: (1) His protection of the three men in a blazing furnace (see Daniel 3); (2) His writing on the wall and Daniel's interpretation of it (see Daniel 5); (3) His provision of safety for Daniel in a lions' den (see Daniel 6); and (4) supernatural prophecies (see Daniel 2; 7; 8; 9:24–12:13).

INTERPRETIVE CHALLENGES

The main challenges involve passages about future tribulation and kingdom promises. Although the use of imperial Aramaic and archeological discoveries have confirmed the early writing date, some skeptical interpreters, unwilling to acknowledge fulfilled, supernatural prophecies (there are more than 100 in Daniel 11 alone), place these details in the intertestamental times. They see these prophecies, not as miraculously foretelling the future, but as simply the historical observations of a later writer, who is recording the events of his own day.

According to this scheme, the expectation of the stone and Son of Man in Daniel 2 and 7 were either (1) a mistaken opinion that did not actually come to pass, or (2) the writer being intentionally deceptive. Actually, (1) a future seven-year judgment period, and (2) a literal 1,000-year kingdom after Christ's Second Coming to reign over Israelites and Gentiles are taught. This will be an era before and distinct from the final, absolutely perfect, ultimate state—the new heaven and the new earth with its capital, the New Jerusalem (see Revelation 21–22). The literal interpretation of prophecy leads to the premillennial perspective.

Many other aspects of interpretation will also challenge readers, such as interpreting numbers; identifying the "one like a Son of Man"; determining whether Antiochus is historical or the Antichrist of the far future in 8:19–23; explaining the "seventy sevens" in 9:24–27; and deciding whether Antiochus of 11:21–35 continues in 11:36–45, or whether it is the future Antichrist.

THE BOOK OF ESTHER

Esther and Ruth are the only Old Testament books named after women. Like the Song of Solomon, Obadiah, and Nahum, the New Testament writers do not quote or allude to Esther. The name Esther comes either from either the Persian word *star* or possibly from *Ishtar,* the name of the Babylonian love goddess.

Author and Date

The author remains unknown, though Mordecai, Ezra, and Nehemiah have been suggested. Whoever penned Esther possessed a detailed knowledge of Persian customs, etiquette, and history, in addition to familiarity with the palace at Shushan. He also exhibited intimate knowledge of the Hebrew calendar and customs, while additionally showing a strong sense of Jewish nationalism. He was possibly a Persian Jew who later moved back to Israel.

The Esther account ends in 473 BC, before Ahasuerus was assassinated (c. 465 BC). Esther 10:2 speaks as though Ahasuerus's reign has been completed, so the earliest possible writing date would be after his reign around the mid-fifth century BC. The latest reasonable date would be prior to 331 BC when Greece conquered Persia.

Background and Setting

The events depicted in Esther took place during the time span between the first return of the Jews after the seventy-year captivity in Babylon under Zerubbabel (c. 538 BC) and the second return led by Ezra (c. 458 BC). The book specifically covers the years 483–473 BC, during the reign of King Ahasuerus of Persia. (Note that *Ahasuerus* represents the Hebrew transliteration of the Persian name *Khshayarsha*, while *Xerxes* represents his Greek name).

Esther and Exodus both chronicle how foreign powers tried to eliminate the Jewish race and how God sovereignly preserved His people in accordance with His covenant promise to Abraham. As a result of God's deliverance, a new annual festival called Purim was initiated in the twelfth month (February/March) to celebrate the nation's survival. Purim became one of two festivals not mandated by Mosaic legislation that were celebrated in Israel.

Historical and Theological Themes

Esther has been accepted as canonical, though the absence of God's name has caused some to doubt its authenticity. (The Greek Septuagint added an extra 107 apocryphal verses to supposedly compensate for this lack.) Rabbis read the Old Testament books of Esther, Song of Solomon, Ruth, Ecclesiastes, and Lamentations in the synagogue on five special occasions during the year—with Esther being read at Purim.

The genesis for the drama between Mordecai (a Benjamite descendant of Saul) and Haman (an Agagite) goes back 1,000 years when the Jews left Egypt and were attacked by the Amalekites (see Exodus 17:8–16). God pronounced His curse on the Amalekites, which resulted in their total elimination as a people. Although Saul received orders to kill all the Amalekites, including their king Agag, he disobeyed and incurred God's displeasure, leaving Samuel to hack Agag into pieces (see 1 Samuel 15).

The events in Esther took place 550 years after the death of Agag, but neither Haman nor Mordecai had forgotten the tribal feud that still smoldered in their souls. This explains why Mordecai refused to bow down to Haman and why Haman so viciously attempted to exterminate the Jewish race. As expected, God's prophecy that he would extinguish the Amalekites and God's promise to preserve the Jews prevailed.

Esther could be compared to a chess game, with God and Satan (as invisible players) moving real kings, queens, and nobles. Ever since the Fall, Satan had tried to sever God's relationship with His human creation and disrupt His covenant promises with Israel. At one point, Christ's line through the tribe of Judah had been murderously reduced to Joash alone, who was rescued and preserved (see 2 Chronicles 22:10–12). Later, Herod slaughtered the infants of Bethlehem, thinking Christ was among them (see Matthew 2:16). Finally, Satan entered Judas, who then betrayed Christ to the Jews and the Romans (see Luke 22:3–6).

God is everywhere apparent in Esther as the One who opposed and foiled Satan's diabolical schemes by providential intervention. His love for Israel is nowhere more apparent than in this dramatic rescue of His people from pending elimination. "Behold, He who keeps Israel shall neither slumber nor sleep" (Psalm 121:4).

INTERPRETIVE CHALLENGES

The most obvious question raised by the book of Esther is why God is nowhere mentioned (as in the Song of Solomon). Nor does the writer or any participant refer to the Law of God, the Levitical sacrifices, worship, or prayer. Yet Esther represents the classic illustration of God's providence as He, the unseen power, controls everything for His purpose. There are no obvious miracles in Esther, but the preservation of Israel through providential control of every event and person reveals the omniscience and omnipotence of Jehovah.

A second question is why Mordecai and Esther were so secular in their lifestyles. Esther did not seem to have the zeal for holiness that Daniel did, and she and Mordecai kept their Jewish heritage a secret. The Law of God is seemingly absent (unlike Ezra) and neither Esther nor Mordecai seemed to have a heart for Jerusalem (unlike Nehemiah).

To answer this question, we must remember this short book does not record everything. Perhaps Mordecai and Esther actually possessed a deeper faith than is apparent here. Second, even godly Nehemiah did not mention his God when talking to King Artaxerxes. Third, the Jewish festivals, which provided structure for worship, had been lost long before Esther. Fourth, it is possible the anti-Jewish letter written by the Samaritans to Ahasuerus several years earlier had frightened Esther and Mordecai. Fifth, the evil intentions of Haman did not just surface when Mordecai refused to bow down. Sixth, Esther did identify with her Jewish heritage at a most appropriate time.

Yet the nagging question of why Esther and Mordecai did not seem to have the same kind of open devotion to God as Daniel did remains. Further, Nehemiah's prayer seems to indicate a spiritual lethargy among the Jewish exiles in Susa (see Nehemiah 1:5–11). Ultimately, God must resolve this issue, for He alone knows human hearts.

Timeline of Daniel and Esther

Date (BC)	Event
605	Nebuchadnezzar takes Daniel captive.
603	Daniel interprets Nebuchadnezzar's dream.
586	The Babylonians destroy Jerusalem.
580	Daniel's friends are kept safe in the fiery furnace.
550	Belshazzar assumes the throne in Babylon.
539	Babylon falls to Cyrus of Persia.
538	The Jews are allowed to return from Persia to Jerusalem.
537	Daniel is kept safe in the lions' den.
521–486	Darius I reigns in Persia.
486–485	Ahasuerus reigns in Persia.
483	Ahasuerus holds his banquet.
479	Esther goes to Ahasuerus.
474	Haman plots against the Jews; Mordecai is honored.
458	Ezra leads a group of Jews back to Jerusalem.

Note: Dates are approximate.

CARRIED INTO CAPTIVITY

Daniel 1:1–21

DRAWING NEAR

What is the most difficult situation you have ever had to face? What did that situation reveal about your faith in God?

_____

_____

_____

THE CONTEXT

From the foundation of the nation of Israel, God warned His people that if they turned away from Him and served pagan idols, He would send foreign enemies to destroy their cities and take them captive (see Leviticus 26). Nevertheless, the Israelites persisted for generations in running after false gods and indulging in all manner of immoral behavior. The Lord was patient, offering His people opportunities to repent, but eventually the time came for Him to discipline him.

In 722 BC, the Assyrians overran Israel and carried the people into captivity, leaving only the tribe of Judah living around Jerusalem. Judah vacillated between obedience and idolatry for a time, but eventually they, too, were taken into captivity by Babylon. This captivity took place in several stages. The first group to be taken to Babylon included Daniel in 605 BC, and it is at that time that our study opens. When Daniel was taken away, he was a young man, probably around fifteen years old. He found himself in a foreign culture, surrounded by powerful slave-masters who worshiped false gods and ate foods that were forbidden to God's people.

From a human perspective, there would seem to be no hope. A young man, cut off from his people and powerless to resist the forces around him, must certainly compromise his standards or be destroyed. Yet Daniel firmly believed that God was in complete control of his circumstances. He trusted that the Lord would always be faithful to His people if they would just be faithful to His Word. Daniel, therefore, resolved in his heart to obey God, and the Lord rewarded his obedience with stunning success.

KEYS TO THE TEXT

Read Daniel 1:1–21, noting the key words and phrases indicated below.

> CARRIED TO BABYLON: *Daniel relates how King Nebuchadnezzar's army besieged Judah as the Lord carried out discipline on His people. Daniel and others were carried into captivity.*

1:1. THE THIRD YEAR OF THE REIGN OF JEHOIAKIM: This was the third year by Babylonian dating (606–605 BC), which did not count a king's initial (accession) year, but began with the following year. So the "third year" is in harmony with the same year labeled as "fourth" by the Judean system of dating (see Jeremiah 46:2). Jehoiakim was one of the last kings of Judah who ruled when Nebuchadnezzar first plundered Jerusalem.

2. THE LORD GAVE . . . JUDAH INTO HIS HAND: The Lord had warned His people that He would send them into captivity if they did not obey His commands (see Leviticus 26), yet the people of Israel (and Judah after the nation of Israel split in two) persisted in idolatry and all manner of disobedience. (Israel had been taken into captivity more than a hundred years earlier.)

SHINAR: That is, Babylon, located in present-day Iraq.

TO THE HOUSE OF HIS GOD: The Babylonians worshiped a number of false gods, notably one called Bel (also known as Marduk or Merodach). King Nebuchadnezzar was effectively making an offering to his false god, thanking him for the victory that (he believed) his god had given him over the God of Judah. However, as we will see in both Daniel and Esther, the Lord was not defeated or even faced with a setback. He was absolutely sovereign over the affairs of people and of nations, and this captivity was part of His plan.

TRAINING PROGRAM: The king sets aside a group of gifted young men and grooms them for his special service. Powerful jobs are offered, and there is likely much competition.

4. YOUNG MEN IN WHOM THERE WAS NO BLEMISH: Nebuchadnezzar's stipulation referred primarily to the physical appearance and accomplishments of the young men. Qualifications included being free from physical blemish or handicap, handsome, mentally sharp, and socially poised and polished for representing the leadership. The Old Testament law also called for sacrifices in which there was "no blemish," which provides a picture of God's final sacrifice for sins: Jesus Christ, the holy Lamb of God, in whom there was no sin.

WHOM THEY MIGHT TEACH: The Babylonians intended to indoctrinate the young men into the teachings of their culture and pagan religions. Daniel and his friends, however, would prove to be strong in the Lord and able to assimilate to the fashions and learning of the Babylonians without taking on any of their pagan beliefs.

THE LANGUAGE AND LITERATURE OF THE CHALDEANS: The Chaldeans (or Babylonians) and Assyrians had produced a large body of literature in all genres, much as Great Britain did for modern Western literature. The language commonly spoken in Babylon was Aramaic, which remained a universal tongue in the ancient Near East until the time of Christ.

5. A DAILY PROVISION OF THE KING'S DELICACIES: These promising young men lived and ate well, literally enjoying the fare of kings. Yet the term *delicacies* in the Old Testament generally carried a negative connotation, indicating self-indulgence in the finer things of the world. King Nebuchadnezzar undoubtedly meant to earn the favor and loyalty of these young men by seducing them to abandon their foreign ways and embrace Babylonian culture and paganism.

7. THE CHIEF OF THE EUNUCHS GAVE NAMES: The act of giving someone a new name demonstrates complete authority over that person, so in this instance Nebuchadnezzar was establishing his authority over the young men of Judah. But more than this, the names also indicated the young men would become subject to the gods of the Babylonians. Their Hebrew names were based on faith in the Lord: "God is my judge" (Daniel), "Yahweh is gracious" (Hananiah), "Yahweh is my helper" (Azariah), and "Who is like the Lord" (Mishael). Their new names, however, invoked the names of the false Babylonian gods: Bel, Marduk, and Nebo.

BELTESHAZZAR . . . SHADRACH . . . MESHACH . . . ABED-NEGO: Belteshazzar means "Bel protect the king," Shadrach means "command of Aku" (another Babylonian god), Meshach means "who is what Aku Is," and Abed-nego means "servant of Nego," also called Nebo, a god of vegetation.

A STEADFAST PURPOSE: Daniel determines in advance that he will not disobey God's commands, even if it sets him apart from the culture around him—and even if he must disobey the king.

8. DANIEL PURPOSED IN HIS HEART: Daniel was determined to be faithful to God even before he was faced with making any decision. The Hebrew might be translated, "he fixed his will" or firmly resolved himself on that course of action.

WOULD NOT DEFILE HIMSELF: The king's diet included food that had been sacrificed to idols as well as things the Lord had commanded His people to not eat (such as pork). To eat such things would have publicly identified Daniel with the false gods, and it would have placed him contrary to God's commands. Moses had taken this stand (see Hebrews 11:24–26), as had the psalmist (see Psalm 119:115). Daniel and his friends were determined not to be seduced into pagan practices, even while obeying the king's will whenever it did not conflict with God's Word. They were striving to be in the world but not of the world (see John 17:14–16).

9. GOD HAD BROUGHT DANIEL INTO THE FAVOR AND GOODWILL: It is interesting that this verse does not read, "Daniel *found* favor," but that God specifically *brought* him into favor. Daniel had suffered a tremendous calamity when he was carried forcibly away to Babylon, yet God had not abandoned him. The captivity was part of His deliberate plan, and He was using those who remained faithful to accomplish His purposes. All that was required of Daniel and his friends was for them to remain obedient to His Word, and the Lord would take care of the details.

10. I FEAR MY LORD THE KING: We should understand that Daniel also respected King Nebuchadnezzar as the Lord's appointed leader over Babylon, under whose authority the Lord had placed him and the others from Judah. He was, however, in a difficult predicament, as he wanted to obey the king's edicts while not disobeying God's Word. Yet the Lord was in control, and He would reward Daniel's faithfulness.

THEN YOU WOULD ENDANGER MY HEAD BEFORE THE KING: Daniel's request also placed the chief of the eunuchs in a difficult position. He was responsible to carry out King Nebuchadnezzar's plan for grooming these young men for positions of responsibility, and he feared that a change of diet might prove detrimental. However, the Lord had already given Daniel favor in this man's eyes, and the eunuch decided to embrace Daniel's proposal.

12. PLEASE TEST YOUR SERVANTS FOR TEN DAYS: Daniel did not simply go to the steward with a complaint and demand a change of diet. Rather, he went with a specific plan in mind that would offer the steward a way out of his dilemma while also enabling Daniel and his friends to obey God's Word. This allowed Daniel to demonstrate his respect for the king's wishes while also publicly declaring his obedience to the Lord.

VEGETABLES TO EAT AND WATER TO DRINK: The Hebrew construction here suggests that the "vegetables" may also have included grain products. The young men chose to drink water rather than the king's wine because it, too, was probably offered to idols prior to being placed on the table.

13. THEN LET OUR APPEARANCE BE EXAMINED: Daniel was fully confident that obedience to God's commands would lead to healthful results. He had no doubt that the Lord would bring the experiment to a successful conclusion.

AS YOU SEE FIT, SO DEAL WITH YOUR SERVANTS: Daniel once again reiterated his willingness to submit to earthly authority. He took pains to make it clear that he wanted to obey both God and the king, and his alternate suggestion was intended merely to remove the conflict.

GOD TAKES CARE OF THE DETAILS: Daniel's faithfulness to God's Word bears remarkable fruit, and the Lord blesses His servants.

15. BETTER AND FATTER IN FLESH: God gave success to Daniel's proposal and made the four young men healthier and fitter than their peers—and in the brief period of just ten days! This was a remarkably short time for a change of

diet to produce visible results, but Daniel's faith and obedience gave God the opportunity to work a miracle for the entire court of Nebuchadnezzar to witness.

17. GOD GAVE THEM KNOWLEDGE AND SKILL: All gifts and blessings come directly from the hand of God, including those innate talents and abilities with which humans are born. The Lord blessed Daniel and his friends with skill and success in all their endeavors under their captivity. Their faithfulness to God's commands permitted Him to demonstrate His faithfulness to them.

DANIEL HAD UNDERSTANDING IN ALL VISIONS AND DREAMS: In addition to his intellectual prowess, the Lord also gave Daniel a specific gift for interpreting visions and dreams. God had a job for Daniel to do, and He provided the skills he would need to accomplish it.

19. THE KING INTERVIEWED THEM: This was an important job interview, as the king was examining all the young men to find out which were most fit to serve him in demanding official capacities. It is quite likely there was fierce competition within the ranks of the young men—though the Scripture text does not bring this out—since all would have been vying for the most important positions.

20. HE FOUND THEM TEN TIMES BETTER: It is significant to remember that Daniel and his friends did nothing special whatsoever in preparing for their interview with the king—nothing except to steadfastly obey God's commands. It was not their special diet that enabled them to vastly excel over everyone else in the king's service but God's blessing of gifts and success. Daniel took care to obey God, and the Lord took care of the rest.

21. FIRST YEAR OF KING CYRUS: Cyrus of Persia would conquer Babylon in 539 BC. Cyrus'"third year," mentioned in Daniel 10:1, is the latest historical year the prophet mentions.

UNLEASHING THE TEXT

1) Why did God allow the people of Judah to be taken captive? If you had been Daniel, how would your slavery have affected your view of God?

_____

_____

_____

2) What qualities did the Babylonians look for when selecting candidates among the Jews? What was the purpose of Nebuchadnezzar's plan to set apart the young men?

_____

_____

_____

3) Why did Daniel not want to eat the diet of the king? What would the implications have been if he had done so? If you had been in his place, what would you have done?

_____

_____

_____

4) What does it mean that "Daniel purposed in his heart" not to defile himself (verse 8)? How is this done? Why is it important?

_____

_____

_____

EXPLORING THE MEANING

The Lord may allow hardship, but He is still in control. The nations of Israel and Judah had persisted in idolatry and disobedience to God's commands, and the time had come for God to send His discipline against them. The nation of Israel was carried into captivity by the Assyrians, and years later the people of Judah suffered the same fate at the hands of the Babylonians. The walls of Jerusalem were torn down, the temple was razed, and the people's homes were plundered and burned. Those who survived became prisoners of war and were carried away to a distant land—a land whose people neither feared God nor knew His Word.

Yet the Lord was still in control over all these circumstances, and He had not abandoned His people. He was sending a time of suffering to the Jews, but that hardship was intended for their purification and their strengthening, and it was all part of His plan. Furthermore, the Lord promised through His prophets that it would only be for a limited time. At the end of seventy years, God would call some of His people to return and rebuild Jerusalem.

Throughout the course of these studies, we will see that God is in complete control over all circumstances in the lives of His people—even during those times when life seems to be spiraling out of control. Just as He directed the steps of Daniel and his friends, He will do so in our lives as well. As Samuel's mother, Hannah, said, "The LORD kills and makes alive; He brings down to the grave and brings up. The LORD makes poor and makes rich; He brings low and lifts up. He raises the poor from the dust and lifts the beggar from the ash heap, to set them among princes and make them inherit the throne of glory. For the pillars of the earth are the LORD's, and He has set the world upon them. He will guard the feet of His saints" (1 Samuel 2:6–9).

We must resolve in our hearts to obey God's Word. Daniel and his three friends were young men, probably in their mid-teens, when the Babylonians carried them away into exile. We can only imagine the temptations and fears they faced as they found themselves living in a pagan culture with strange gods, traditions, and practices. They were wrenched from their homes and family and sent far away from those who knew and worshiped the true God of Israel. It would have been easy in such circumstances for them to fall into despair, hopelessness, and any number of sinful practices.

However, Daniel instead demonstrated great wisdom by making a firm resolution in his heart to obey God's commands, whatever might come. He recognized he was faced with temptations and threats that would lead him into behavior unpleasing to God, and he determined in advance not to be led astray. For him, this meant not eating the food set before him, as it included meats and drink that had been sacrificed to idols and various "unclean" meats—things the Lord had expressly forbidden His people to consume.

Life is filled with situations that test our resolve, offer temptations that cause us to stray from God's commands, and exert pressures that compel us to compromise with the world's standard. Fortunately, when we give our lives over to Christ, God gives us His Holy Spirit to empower us to resist and stand firm against those pressures and temptations—but we must still be resolved to act in obedience. The time to make a firm resolution to walk in God's ways and set one's heart resolutely to obey the Lord is before the time of temptation comes. As Solomon wrote, "Keep your heart with all diligence, for out of it spring the issues of life" (Proverbs 4:23).

Christians must submit to human authorities. Daniel was in a difficult situation. The Lord had commanded him to abstain from certain types of meat that were considered unclean and to refrain from eating anything that had been offered as a sacrifice to a pagan idol. However, once in Babylon, he found himself faced with a steady diet that included both types of forbidden food. What was worse, he had been commanded by the king himself to eat those foods! He seemed to be forced to choose to either obey God but disobey the king, or follow the king's orders but do what God and the law had commanded him not to do.

However, as we have seen, there was in fact a third option. Daniel found a way to submit himself to the king's authority while still obeying God's commands, and the Lord blessed him by giving resounding success to his plan. What underlay Daniel's plan was a genuine respect for the human authorities God had placed him under. His motive was to obey both king and God, not to rebel against human authority under the guise of submitting to the Lord. God commands us to submit to both Him and our earthly authorities, and in most cases it is possible to do both at the same time.

We will see in later studies this is not *absolutely* always the case, but even in a difficult situation Daniel found a way to obey both God and king. This is the Lord's will for all His people, whatever culture or authority they may find themselves under—in society, at work, at church, and in the home. In all settings, we are to obey society's laws, follow company policies, and submit ourselves willingly to those whom the Lord has placed in authority. As Paul reminds us, "Let every soul be subject to the governing authorities. For there is no authority except from God, and God appoints the authorities that exist. Therefore whoever resists the authority resists the ordinance of God, and those who resist will bring judgment on themselves" (Romans 13:1–2).

Reflecting on the Text

5) What part did God play in the events of this chapter? What part did Daniel play? What brought about Daniel's stunning success?

_____

_____

_____

6) Why did Daniel offer an alternate plan for his diet? Why did he not simply refuse to eat? What might the results have been if he had responded differently?

_____

_____

_____

7) What evidence did Daniel have that God was in control? What factor might have tempted him to lose heart? How might you have reacted?

_____

_____

_____

8) When have you faced a situation where you felt coerced into disobeying God's Word? What did you do? What were the results?

_____

_____

_____

PERSONAL RESPONSE

9) To what human authorities do you find it difficult to submit? Why? What is your usual response? How might Daniel respond in your circumstances?

_____

_____

_____

_____

10) Is there an area of God's Word in which you are presently compromising with the world's teachings? What will you do this week to change that?

_____

_____

_____

_____

2

A DISTURBING DREAM
Daniel 2:1–49

DRAWING NEAR

What recurring dreams or nightmares did you have when you were young? What recurring dreams or nightmares do you have now?

_____

_____

_____

THE CONTEXT

As we have seen, Babylon was the most powerful nation in the world of Daniel's day, having already demonstrated its sovereignty over Judah (eventually destroying it completely), just as Assyria had done to Israel more than 100 years earlier. Assyria had been the major world power in that time, just as Egypt had been previously. The nations of the world continued to rise and fall—to gain ascendancy only to be overpowered by another—and Babylon would be no exception to that principle.

King Nebuchadnezzar was the most powerful man in the world, yet his great kingdom would not last forever. The Lord made that clear to him one night by sending him a strange dream in which he saw a giant statue of a man composed of a variety of metals. Nebuchadnezzar knew the dream had deep significance, but he could not understand what it meant. However, for the king that was not a problem. Nebuchadnezzar had a large group of advisors he kept on hand for just such a purpose as this—to interpret prophetic dreams and explain divine mysteries.

These Babylonian advisors were like the scientific and medical experts of our day, specially trained in the vast learning of humankind. They were the most learned men in their fields and claimed to understand the stars, the inner mysteries of the human psyche, and the ways of the gods. Yet Nebuchadnezzar had some doubts about the real extent of their skills, especially when it came to interpreting a prophetic dream, and so he set before them a test: "If you do not make known the dream to me, and its interpretation, you shall be cut in pieces" (Daniel 2:5). As it would turn out, his doubts were well founded.

KEYS TO THE TEXT

Read Daniel 2:1–49, noting the key words and phrases indicated below.

> NEBUCHADNEZZAR'S DREAM: *King Nebuchadnezzar has a troubling dream, and he tests his wise men to find the correct interpretation. The wise men, however, cannot meet his demands.*

2:1. IN THE SECOND YEAR OF NEBUCHADNEZZAR'S REIGN: Differences in the method of counting a king's years of reign have caused some confusion on exact dates, but this event probably occurred after the three years of Daniel's training were ended, in 603 BC.

HIS SPIRIT WAS SO TROUBLED: This was not the first time God used dreams to warn people of coming events. He used dreams to encourage Joseph (Genesis 37) and to warn Pharaoh (Genesis 41), and later we will see how He also used dreams in the life of Esther. King Nebuchadnezzar was troubled because he recognized that his dreams had more significance than just the idle fancies of sleep, but he was at a loss to understand what they meant.

2. THE MAGICIANS, THE ASTROLOGERS, THE SORCERERS, AND THE CHALDEANS: These men claimed to be "dream experts" who were knowledgeable in medicine and such. The reality is that they practiced the occult arts, including sorcery and astrological pursuits that God had forbidden for his people (see Deuteronomy 18:10–12). Chaldea was another name for Babylon, but in this

usage the word *Chaldeans* refers to men who were learned in the knowledge and literature of the Babylonians.

TO TELL THE KING HIS DREAMS: Notice the king summoned his experts to tell him what was *in* his dreams, not merely to interpret them. This demonstrates the uselessness of predicting the future based on interpretations of dreams. Unless there is a prophet with divine revelation from God, there is no way to rightly interpret a dream.

4. TELL YOUR SERVANTS THE DREAM: This certainly seems a natural request; one can hardly be expected to interpret a dream without first being told what the dream is! But Nebuchadnezzar wanted to discover how much his expert really could be relied on in something as important as this.

5. YOU SHALL BE CUT IN PIECES: This judgment may seem unreasonable and harsh at first glance, yet it was not entirely unjust. The magicians and astrologers claimed to have insight into the minds of "the gods," which meant they claimed their interpretations were inspired.

7. LET THE KING TELL HIS SERVANTS THE DREAM: The magicians knew the king was calling their bluff, and they were understandably filled with terror because they knew they could not live up to their false claims of God-given insight.

8. I KNOW FOR CERTAIN THAT YOU WOULD GAIN TIME: The fear and hesitation of the magicians proved to the king that they could not reveal the truth, and now they were just stalling for time.

9. LYING AND CORRUPT WORDS: It would have been easy enough for the magicians to agree on some abstract interpretation of the dream—if they only knew what it was! Nebuchadnezzar's tactic was both shrewd and wise, as he forced the interpreters to prove their credentials before listening to their interpretation.

11. WHOSE DWELLING IS NOT WITH FLESH: Ironically, this was exactly the point God wanted people of all nations to understand: He *had* chosen to make His dwelling among them and had made Himself available to them (see Isaiah 57:15). He made His presence known through Moses and the nation of Israel, and His plan was ultimately fulfilled through Christ.

DANIEL PRAYS: Daniel and his friends find their lives in jeopardy, but they turn to the Lord in prayer—and God grants their request.

13. THEY SOUGHT DANIEL AND HIS COMPANIONS: Evidently the king's special training for the young men was to groom them for such counsel as was

presently needed. The abysmal failure of the magicians put Daniel's life in danger, as he was considered one of them.

14. WITH COUNSEL AND WISDOM: Once again we find Daniel approaching human authority figures with deference and wisdom. It is possible that he had heard about the king's decree and had time to seek wise counsel with his three godly friends. It is quite certain, however, that the Lord was with him and gave him wisdom, even if he was caught unawares by this sudden summons.

18. SEEK MERCIES FROM THE GOD OF HEAVEN: Daniel and his friends knew exactly what to do in this crisis: pray! The Lord had given Daniel a gift of understanding dreams (see Daniel 1:17), yet Daniel clearly recognized his gift lay in God's hands, not in himself. He trusted that the Lord would be faithful to reveal the dream to him, but he also understood the Lord wanted His people to turn to Him in prayer, asking Him to remember His promises.

21. HE CHANGES THE TIMES AND THE SEASONS: Daniel's prayer of worship addresses an important aspect of God's character: His sovereignty. God is absolutely in control of all earthly affairs, including raising kings and deposing them, and extending to the changes of the seasons.

27. THE SOOTHSAYERS CANNOT DECLARE TO THE KING: Nebuchadnezzar's demands were impossible for any man to fulfill, as only God can fathom the heart of a man and reveal his innermost thoughts. Nebuchadnezzar undoubtedly recognized this and was looking for a man who had a special relationship with God (or with "the gods," as he likely would have understood it).

THE DREAM: *Daniel first describes the king's dream and then gives him the interpretation from God. The final fulfillment will come in the future when Christ returns.*

31. A GREAT IMAGE: That is, a huge statue of a man. The statue was composed of various metals, as listed in the following verses.

32–33: GOLD . . . SILVER . . . BRONZE . . . IRON . . . CLAY: The metals listed gradually decrease in value while increasing in strength. The people of the time used gold, silver, and bronze decoratively for their beauty, but used bronze in weaponry until they superseded it with the stronger (but less attractive) iron. Yet even though the metals increased in strength, they culminated in a mixture of iron and clay, which would be the weakest item in the list. Indeed, iron weakened by clay would have no practical purpose at all.

34. A STONE WAS CUT OUT WITHOUT HANDS: That is, no hands were used in cutting out the stone. This is an image of Christ, also referred to as "a stumbling stone and rock of offense" (Romans 9:33).

35. NO TRACE OF THEM WAS FOUND: The statue of various metals represented the many human kingdoms that have risen and fallen throughout the history of humankind. When Christ finally sets up His millennial kingdom, every governmental system that humans have ever established will be of no account. It will be as though none had ever existed.

37. THE GOD OF HEAVEN HAS GIVEN YOU A KINGDOM, POWER, STRENGTH, AND GLORY: The statue's golden head represented Nebuchadnezzar and the great kingdom of Babylon. According to Daniel's words, there has never been another kingdom as majestic and glorious on the earth. Yet even in giving this grand praise to the king, Daniel made it clear that Nebuchadnezzar's great accomplishments were from God, and there was no room for him to take credit for or pride in his kingdom.

39. BUT AFTER YOU SHALL ARISE ANOTHER KINGDOM: As grand and majestic as Babylon was, it was still only an earthly, human system of government, and as such its days were numbered. No human government will ever last—only the government established by the King of kings and Lord of lords will endure.

40. THE FOURTH KINGDOM SHALL BE AS STRONG AS IRON: The nations represented in the dream were Babylon (gold), Medo-Persia (silver), Greece (bronze), Rome (iron), and a future earthly domain (iron and clay). The Roman Empire was indeed as powerful as iron; its ironclad armies were known as the Iron Legions of Rome. The Roman Empire was known for its ruthless ability to crush any nation that resisted its authority.

42. PARTLY OF IRON AND PARTLY OF CLAY: This picture does in some measure describe the last days of the Roman Empire, when Rome grew unable to control its far-flung dominions. But the complete fulfillment of this dream has yet to take place, as Daniel's further interpretation makes clear. Most scholars view the feet as representing a future revival of the Roman Empire or some human government set up in its style that will rule all or most of the world. The toes are probably the ten kings described in Daniel's later vision (see Daniel 7), which represent ten rulers who will form a confederation in the future. This kingdom will be both powerful and weak and will be the existing world power at the time of Christ's return.

43. THE SEED OF MEN: This seems to suggest the final kingdom will be a heterogeneous mixture of many nations who will not remain loyal to one another when push comes to shove. Yet the phrase "the seed of men" reminds us that whatever form a human government may take, it is still a product of the schemes of men, and as such it cannot endure.

44. A KINGDOM WHICH SHALL NEVER BE DESTROYED: This will be the millennial kingdom, established by Christ at His second advent. It will continue on earth for a thousand years (a millennium), after which will come the final judgment and His eternal heavenly kingdom (see Revelation 20). God will establish His kingdom, ruled by His Son, and it will endure throughout all eternity without interruption. It will not be superseded by "another people," as was the case with each of the nations in the dream, but will instead crush and obliterate all forms of human government that have been attempted throughout the history of the world.

45. THE DREAM IS CERTAIN: Nebuchadnezzar's dream was a prophecy sent from God, and as such its fulfillment was—and is—absolutely certain. Most of it, in fact, has already come to pass and is ancient history to us, as the empires of Persia, Greece, and Rome have long since faded away. But the vision of God's future kingdom under His Son will absolutely come to pass, and nothing can prevent its fulfillment.

46. NEBUCHADNEZZAR FELL ON HIS FACE: Daniel had accomplished what no human could by describing the king's dream and interpreting its meaning. Nebuchadnezzar recognized that no human agency could have accomplished this miracle, and this offering was presumably intended for the Lord, not for Daniel (who would have instantly refused it).

47. TRULY YOUR GOD IS THE GOD OF GODS: Daniel's faithfulness made it clear to the king that his dream had been interpreted correctly only through the power of God. As a result, the king himself publicly acknowledged that the Lord is the King of kings.

48. HE MADE HIM RULER OVER THE WHOLE PROVINCE OF BABYLON: The Lord had used Joseph in a similar manner in Egypt more than 1,000 years earlier (see Genesis 41), and in both cases His plan was for the greater good of His people. God holds complete control over all events of our personal lives, but His plan extends to all people throughout time and into eternity. "A man's heart plans his way, but the Lord directs his steps" (Proverbs 106:9).

UNLEASHING THE TEXT

1) Why did King Nebuchadnezzar insist that his wise men describe his dream? What did this reveal about his expectations concerning its interpretation?

_____

_____

_____

2) Why were the wise men unable to describe the dream? What did this reveal about the source of their powers?

_____

_____

_____

3) How did Daniel respond when asked to go before the king? What did this reveal about his character?

_____

_____

_____

4) What did the dream represent? What did God reveal through the dream about the various kingdoms? About the final kingdom?

_____

_____

_____

EXPLORING THE MEANING

Jesus will one day return to earth and establish His eternal kingdom. Nebuchadnezzar's dream pictured a succession of world powers, beginning with his own reign in Babylon and stretching out more than 500 years through the age of the Roman Empire. Those world powers formed the body of the statue in the king's dream, from the golden head of Babylon down through the iron legs of Rome. Each of those nations has long since faded into ancient history, yet one part of that dream has yet to be fulfilled: the feet of clay, smashed by a rock hurled from heaven.

That rock is Jesus, and the statue's feet represent a world kingdom that is yet to be established. At some future date, Christ will return and take control over the earth, abolishing all forms of human government and establishing His throne over all peoples and dominions. He will take up His scepter as King of kings and Lord of lords, and all the nations of the earth will bow before Him. He will maintain this earthly kingdom for a thousand years (called the millennium), after which He will bring about a new heaven and a new earth (see Revelation 20–21).

As Daniel told Nebuchadnezzar, these events are certain and sure. As truly as the dream was fulfilled concerning the kingdoms of the past, so it shall also be fulfilled concerning the events of the future. Those who acknowledge Jesus now as Lord of their lives will be resurrected to rule with Him in His eternal kingdom—but those who refuse His gift of salvation will rise again in the final resurrection and face His judgment of eternal condemnation. The time of salvation is now, as Scripture warns us. "[God] says: 'In an acceptable time I have heard you, and in the day of salvation I have helped you.' Behold, now is the accepted time; behold, now is the day of salvation" (2 Corinthians 6:2).

The wisdom of this world cannot explain the truths of God. King Nebuchadnezzar had a dream that he could not understand. He normally would have turned to his magicians and counselors for an explanation, but on this occasion he realized the wise men of his age might try to cover their ignorance by inventing an interpretation that would be difficult to prove or disprove. So the king demanded that his counselors begin by first describing the dream itself, which, of course, would be impossible for any man to accomplish.

Yet because God—and not any human agencies—had sent the dream, it was an easy matter for the Lord to tell Nebuchadnezzar *both* the dream and its interpretation. It is significant He chose to do this, not through the great learning of men, but through His obedient servant Daniel. Human wisdom cannot comprehend the mind of God. The world prides itself on great learning and advances in the fields of science, medicine, physics, and biology, but no field of human study or endeavor can reveal the eternal truths of God.

Only God can reveal Himself to humanity, and He has chosen to do so through His Word and His Son. The Bible encapsulates the truth of God in written form, but Jesus Christ embodied the person of God in human form. To know Jesus is to know the mind of God. On the other hand, placing one's faith in modern science and man's intellect is like Nebuchadnezzar trusting in his wise men. As Paul wrote, "Let no one deceive himself. If anyone among you seems to be wise in this age, let him become a fool that he may become wise. For the wisdom of this world is foolishness with God" (1 Corinthians 3:18–19).

God reveals Himself to those who seek Him. Nebuchadnezzar's astrologers and magicians were filled with terror when the king commanded them to describe his dream, for they recognized no human could ever accomplish such a thing. "There is no other who can tell it to the king except the gods," they cried, "whose dwelling is not with flesh" (Daniel 2:11). They did not trust the Lord, and so, of course, they did not turn to God for guidance.

Daniel knew the magicians were partly right, for the correct interpretation was only available from God and not "the gods" whom the magicians served. Daniel had no way of knowing if the Lord would indeed reveal the dream to him, but he and his friends knew their only hope was to trust in God, who was in control of the situation. So Daniel sought the Lord in prayer and trusted that God would guide him through this trial.

As a point of consideration, it is helpful for us to think about how God reveals Himself to people today. As stated in the previous principle, God cannot be known by any means except a saving faith in His Son, Jesus Christ. Paul explained this truth to the wise men of his day: "[God] has made from one blood every nation of men to dwell on all the face of the earth, and has determined their pre-appointed times and the boundaries of their dwellings, so that they should seek the Lord, in the hope that they might grope for Him and find Him, though He is not far from each one of us; for in Him we live and move and have our being" (Acts 17:26–28).

REFLECTING ON THE TEXT

5) Why was Christ pictured in the dream as a rock "cut out of the mountain without hands" (Daniel 2:45)? Why did His kingdom smash the statue to dust?

_____

_____

_____

6) What "experts" would likely be called to interpret such a dream today? How do you think they would fare?

_____

_____

_____

7) Why did God reserve the interpretation of the dream for Daniel? Why did He not reveal it to the magicians and astrologers?

_____

_____

_____

8) What is revealed about the character of God in this chapter? What attributes of God are highlighted in this chapter?

_____

_____

_____

PERSONAL RESPONSE

9) Have you thought about where you stand before God? Have you considered the implications if you refuse to acknowledge Christ as your Savior? If you don't accept Christ as Savior and King, how does this affect your involvement in His coming kingdom?

_____

_____

_____

10) When confronted with a difficult situation, do you generally turn first to the wisdom of the world or to God's Word? What would Daniel do in a similar situation?

_____

_____

_____

3

THE FIERY TRIAL
Daniel 3:1–30

DRAWING NEAR

What are some situations today in which Christians would be called to stand up for God and refuse to obey an earthly authority?

_____

_____

_____

THE CONTEXT

We previously met Daniel's three friends Hananiah, Mishael, and Azariah—whose names had been changed to Shadrach, Meshach, and Abed-Nego—when they refused to eat the king's food that had been offered to idols. After Daniel correctly interpreted the king's dream, these three friends were promoted to positions of responsibility in Babylon, while "Daniel sat in the gate of the king" (Daniel 2:49), or in the king's royal court.

Approximately twenty years passed, and these three young men grew into adults. The Lord had blessed His faithful servants with success, and everything appeared to be going well for the men. They were important members of the court. They served the most powerful monarch on earth in a city that was world-renowned for its beauty and man-made wonders. Who would want to rock the boat in such a situation? Leave well enough alone, as the world's motto goes. Just go with the flow and don't draw attention to yourself.

But what do godly people do when the civil authorities command them to disobey the Word of God? Believers are commanded to submit to human authority, but what happens when that authority defies God? This is precisely the situation that arose for these three men when the king constructed a gigantic statue and commanded them to bow down and worship it. Shadrach, Meshach, and Abed-Nego were forced to choose whom to obey—God or man—and that choice would bring dire consequences.

However, as we will also see in this study, God remains ever faithful to those who obey His Word. He would honor the righteous choice these three men made and miraculously deliver them from their fiery trial.

KEYS TO THE TEXT

Read Daniel 3:1–30, noting the key words and phrases indicated below.

> *THE GOLDEN IMAGE: Nebuchadnezzar builds a statue that is somewhat reminiscent of the one he had dreamed about previously—except this time he commands people to worship it.*

1. NEBUCHADNEZZAR THE KING: The events in this chapter of Daniel occur around 580 BC.

HEIGHT WAS SIXTY CUBITS AND ITS WIDTH SIX CUBITS: A cubit was eighteen to twenty inches in length, depending on whether the measurements were Israelite or Babylonian. The statue was between ninety and 100 feet tall by nine or ten feet wide. The image of the man probably stood atop a large pedestal, which would have made the statue itself of normal human proportions. We are not told whose image it was. Perhaps it was Nebuchadnezzar himself, or perhaps an image of Nabu, a false deity worshiped in Babylon (the first part of Nebuchadnezzar's name).

HE SET IT UP IN THE PLAIN OF DURA: Nebuchadnezzar's statue is reminiscent of the dream he had previously that depicted the form of a man made of gold, silver, bronze, iron, and clay. However, that image represented Babylon and the kingdoms to follow, while Nebuchadnezzar's statue seems to imply there would be no other kingdoms to follow his "golden reign." The giant statue standing alone in a plain is also reminiscent of the Tower of Babel (see Genesis 11), which was another man-made object intended to declare the glory of human accomplishments.

3. THE IMAGE THAT KING NEBUCHADNEZZAR HAD SET UP: This phrase is used frequently in this chapter to emphasize the fact a man-made object was being raised up for people to worship.

5. YOU SHALL FALL DOWN AND WORSHIP THE GOLD IMAGE: Here is where the king's law transgressed the laws of God. God's people are commanded to obey their earthly authorities, but there can come a time when those authorities command God's people to disobey His Word. At that point, their authority ceases to be binding.

6. WHOEVER DOES NOT FALL DOWN AND WORSHIP: It is important to remember that in the views of the ancient Near East, such a law would not have been considered tyrannical. The pagan nations believed that one could freely offer homage to one deity while remaining faithful to another. So, for example, a worshiper of Baal might not feel any compunction about also bowing in worship before this idol. However, God commanded His people to worship Him alone and to refrain from bowing before any false idols. This is why the Jews would have stood out as unique and rebellious in their refusal to bow before Nebuchadnezzar's image.

REFUSING TO BOW DOWN: Daniel's three friends—Shadrach, Meshach, and Abed-Nego—refuse to bow down before the statue. Their faith is about to be put to the test.

8. CERTAIN CHALDEANS . . . ACCUSED THE JEWS: The Chaldeans—the magicians and so-called wise men we met in the previous study—accused Daniel's three friends of not obeying the king's order. The Hebrew phrase translated *accused* could actually be transliterated as "devoured piecemeal." The image is of a ravening beast ripping apart its prey in a feeding frenzy—the Jews were faced with enemies who hated them and sought to chew them up.

12. SHADRACH, MESHACH, AND ABED-NEGO: These are the three friends of Daniel who went through the training process with him when they

were all young men. Like Daniel, they had risen to prominent roles within the kingdom of Babylon.

HAVE NOT PAID DUE REGARD TO YOU: These three men were faced with a difficult situation. The king's law commanded them to disobey God's law, so they were forced to choose whom to obey. By obeying God's commands, they had to disobey the king's commands—which was seen as open rebellion against his authority.

13. IN RAGE AND FURY: It is interesting to see the way in which God's enemies were able to stir up the anger of kings against God's people. Here we find King Nebuchadnezzar flying into a rage and being coerced into throwing loyal servants into the furnace.

14. IS IT TRUE: Nebuchadnezzar at least investigated the truth of the accusations.

15. WHO IS THE GOD WHO WILL DELIVER YOU FROM MY HANDS: Nevertheless, the king was still deceived by his own pride, thinking he was more powerful than Almighty God. He was about to learn the answer to his own question.

16. WE HAVE NO NEED TO ANSWER YOU IN THIS MATTER: That is to say, "We have no defense to offer against these accusations." The three men were not being disrespectful but were acknowledging that the accusations were true—they *had* refused to bow down before the image. They were also letting the king know they had carefully considered their actions and had no need to reconsider now. They were firmly committed to not worshiping the idol.

17. OUR GOD WHOM WE SERVE IS ABLE TO DELIVER US: The men answered the king's rhetorical question by telling him their God was indeed able to save them out of his hand.

18. BUT IF NOT: The men also recognized that the Lord might allow them to die in that fiery furnace. The Lord does sometimes allow His servants to experience suffering—and even death—for His name. Yet the men trusted Him so completely that they were willing to follow His sovereign guidance even to the point of a gruesome death by fire.

BURNING WITH RAGE: Nebuchadnezzar's wrath flares up as hot as his furnace at the men's defiance, and he has them bound and thrown into the flames.

19. NEBUCHADNEZZAR WAS FULL OF FURY: The author emphasized the great wrath of the king, underscoring the fact that his rage was leading him

into sin rather than wise leadership. His wrath was stirred, not by discovering unrighteousness, but by having his will frustrated by the righteousness of the three men that had led them to resist his ungodly demands.

THE EXPRESSION ON HIS FACE CHANGED: The Hebrew word translated *expression* is the same used for the image that Nebuchadnezzar created. The king's pride and willfulness had become an idol in his own life, and he was acting like a stubborn child used to getting his own way.

HEAT THE FURNACE SEVEN TIMES MORE: The king commanded his soldiers to make the furnace as hot as it possibly could be. Ironically, this would have been merciful, as it would have led to a quicker death—if that was what the Lord had willed.

21. THE BURNING FIERY FURNACE: Bricks were the generic building material used in Babylon, and brick kilns were often tall enough for men to walk inside. Little else is known of the furnace, though the details suggest it was a vertical, pipe-like structure (the guards "took up" the men to cast them in). Other details suggest a horizontal structure—the king was seated nearby looking inside (whereas a vertical structure would have been too hot to look down on). Regardless, bricks are baked at 1,600 to 2,000 degrees Fahrenheit.

22. THE FLAME OF THE FIRE KILLED THOSE MEN: King Nebuchadnezzar had boasted that no god could save Daniel's friends from his hand, but the truth was that the king could not save his own men from the hand of God.

> THE FLAMES HAVE NO POWER: *The king suddenly realizes that something is amiss—for there are four men in the furnace instead of three!*

25. THE FOURTH IS LIKE THE SON OF GOD: We are not told whether this was an angel or God Himself. It is quite possible this is a *theophany*, or an appearance of God in human form prior to the birth of Christ. Nebuchadnezzar, of course, was not aware of the triune nature of God—Father, Son, and Holy Spirit—yet even this idolatrous king could not deny the presence and involvement of Almighty God in the lives of these three men.

26. SERVANTS OF THE MOST HIGH GOD: The testimony of these three men, their faith in God, and their open testimony to God's power led a pagan king to publicly acknowledge the Most High God. His words confessed that Israel's God was supreme and able to save those whom He chose out of the hands

of their enemies. Nebuchadnezzar was retracting his earlier boast that no god could save the men from his powerful hand.

CAME FROM THE MIDST OF THE FIRE: The three men had been unable to walk under their own power when they were thrown into the fire, but God's hand of salvation had set them completely free so they could walk out unbound.

27. THE FIRE HAD NO POWER: The powers of this world are powerless against the sovereignty of God, and the dangers God's people face cannot touch them without His permission.

THE SMELL OF FIRE WAS NOT ON THEM: Here is another small picture of the salvation afforded through Christ. Fire is frequently used in Scripture to represent the wrath of God, but Christians are redeemed out of His terrible wrath to the extent there is not even a whiff of judgment on their souls.

28. BLESSED BE THE GOD OF SHADRACH, MESHACH, AND ABED-NEGO: It is significant that Nebuchadnezzar gave glory to God rather than some power the men might have possessed. Their open testimony to God's power and faithfulness left no room for him to think that they had saved themselves, and the king was forced to confess that God was present in their lives.

YIELDED THEIR BODIES: Daniel's three friends had yielded their entire beings to God's sovereign hand, even to the point of submitting to death in order to obey His Word.

29. THE GOD OF SHADRACH, MESHACH, AND ABED-NEGO: Nebuchadnezzar had gained knowledge of the true God through the testimony of Daniel's friends, but he had not yet made Him his own God. We will witness this final conversion in the next study.

UNLEASHING THE TEXT

1) What might have motivated Nebuchadnezzar to create the giant statue? Why would he command people to worship it?

_____

_____

_____

2) How did Nebuchadnezzar discover the unwillingness of the Hebrews to worship the giant idol? How did they respond when confronted?

_____

_____

_____

_____

3) Why did Nebuchadnezzar's anger flare up in this passage? What lay behind his anger? How did it affect his judgment?

_____

_____

_____

_____

4) When is it right to disobey earthly authorities? When is it wrong? How can a Christian discern the difference?

_____

_____

_____

_____

EXPLORING THE MEANING

Man's wrath does not produce God's righteousness. It would appear that Nebuchadnezzar's temper was modeled after his furnaces: fiery! When his magicians asked to know what his dream was before offering an interpretation, he roared, "If you do not make known the dream to me, and its interpretation, you shall be cut in pieces, and your houses shall be made an ash heap" (Daniel 2:5). His rage flared up instantly when his will was thwarted, and his punishments were extreme. Even after he realized that Daniel's friends served Almighty God, he resorted to his old threat of cutting into pieces any who spoke ill of God, making their houses as ash heaps.

The truth is that Nebuchadnezzar's anger was a natural consequence of his pride, not a righteous indignation against defiance or unlawful behavior. It was his pride that led him to create the golden image and command his nation to worship it, and that pride had been offended when Daniel's friends refused to comply. His subsequent anger clouded his judgment, and he ended up defying the God of creation. If the king had humbled himself and cooled his anger, he might have recognized that the men's testimony was true and that his image was nothing more than a false god.

James warned his readers of the deadly trap of human wrath: "So then, my beloved brethren, let every man be swift to hear, slow to speak, slow to wrath; for the wrath of man does not produce the righteousness of God" (James 1:19–20). The Lord had raised Daniel's friends as a witness to the king in order to offer him the chance to hear the truth concerning his idolatrous practices, but the king had refused to listen. Instead, he was quick to speak and quick to indulge his wrath, and as a result he quickly fell into deadly error. When anger flares up, take time to listen and pray. Quick speech can result in negative long-term consequences.

No danger can touch us without God's permission. From the world's perspective, Daniel's three friends must have appeared foolishly overconfident, even self-deluded and out of touch with reality, in their answer to King Nebuchadnezzar. The furnace looming before them was terribly real, as were the flames that leaped and danced out of its mouth. Those flames were so hot they consumed those who got too close, never mind being thrown inside. Yet Shadrach, Meshach, and Abed-Nego remained steadfast in their determination not to bow down.

Those three men knew full well the flames were real, but they also understood those flames were under the sovereign command of their Creator. If God so chose, not a hair on their heads would be singed—which proved to be exactly the case. Yet the men also understood the sovereign Lord of creation could equally choose to let the flames take their natural course, consuming their bodies even as they had consumed the guards. They remained steadfast just the same because they trusted that the Lord's decision in the matter would be the best conclusion, whether they continued to live in this world or passed through death into the eternal presence of their Lord and King.

Their attitude is a model for all believers to follow and cause us to remember that God is absolutely faithful to His children. He will not permit anything to touch us that is not ultimately for our good. As the psalmist wrote, "My help comes from the LORD, who made heaven and earth. He will not allow your foot to be moved; He who keeps you will not slumber. Behold, He who keeps Israel shall neither slumber nor sleep. The LORD is your keeper; the LORD is your shade at your right hand. The sun shall not strike you by day, nor the moon by night. The LORD shall preserve you from all evil; He shall preserve your soul. The LORD shall preserve your going out and your coming in from this time forth, and even forevermore" (Psalm 121:2–8).

Christians bear witness by both word and deed. There is no record that any of King Nebuchadnezzar's subjects spoke out against his construction of the giant statue. As far as we know, there were no organized protests, no people marching in the streets, and no editorials denouncing the project. Neither is there any record of protest against the king's wicked edict that demanded his subjects bow down and worship before that statue. Quite the contrary, in fact: "All the people, nations, and languages fell down and worshiped the gold image which King Nebuchadnezzar had set up" (Daniel 3:7).

Of course, public dissent and organized protests are things of modern times, not the stuff of an absolute monarchy under a king like Nebuchadnezzar. Yet the point is that while Daniel's friends did not march before the king to speak out against his decree, they still bore a powerful witness to the truth of God's Word. They bore that witness visually rather than audibly, and through their deeds more than through their words. They did not hesitate to speak words of truth when the king challenged them on their behavior, but it was their steadfast refusal to bow—their overt actions in the sight of the world around them—that bore the most convincing testimony to God's righteousness.

The principle here is that actions are as important as words. Daniel's friends might have gone about expounding on God's commands against worshiping idols, but if they had then bowed down at the king's command, those words would have lost their power. More than their words, it was the *deeds* of Daniel's friends—their willingness to be thrown into a fiery furnace in obedience to their Lord—that demonstrated the saving power of God. As James noted, "Faith by itself, if it does not have works, is dead" (James 2:17). Daniel's friends verbally expressed their faith in God's power to save, but they also had to *act* on those words before God's power was shown to the world. Christians should be quick to speak the words of God, but if they don't also live by those words, their faith is dead.

REFLECTING ON THE TEXT

5) Put the answer of Daniel's friends (Daniel 3:16–18) into your own words. Why did they refuse to bow down? Why were they so calm in that situation?

_____

_____

_____

6) How did their testimony influence King Nebuchadnezzar? How did it influence the world around them?

_____

_____

_____

7) Why might God have chosen to keep these men alive in the furnace? When in the Bible did He allow His servants to succumb to death? What purposes did He have in each case?

_____

_____

_____

8) Why did a fourth man appear in the furnace with Daniel's friends? What does this teach about God's involvement in your own trials?

_____

_____

_____

PERSONAL RESPONSE

9) What hardships or trials are you dealing with at present? How can the experience of Daniel's friends help you in facing that situation?

_____

_____

_____

10) How do you generally deal with anger? When has your anger hindered God's righteousness? What can you learn from Nebuchadnezzar's example?

_____

_____

_____

4

THE MADNESS OF THE KING
Daniel 4:1-37

DRAWING NEAR

What does it mean that "power corrupts, and absolute power corrupts absolutely?" How have you seen that play out in authority figures?

_____

_____

_____

THE CONTEXT

Babylon was the most powerful and wealthy nation of its day, and the empire extended throughout the Middle East. King Nebuchadnezzar and his father had increased its borders and prestige dramatically, until every nation and language of the day came under its influence. Nebuchadnezzar also undertook many ambitious building projects in his capital city, fortifying Babylon with an extensive system of walls and creating beautiful temples, roads, bridges, palaces, gates, and even a ziggurat. He created a remarkable hanging garden that became one of the seven wonders of the ancient world.

In the process, he also became proud. He stood atop his huge palace walls and gazed out on his realm, quite literally master of all he surveyed, and told himself that he had accomplished it all through his own majesty and might. As we saw in the previous study, he engaged in gross idolatry by constructing a huge statue made of gold, and he commanded all his subjects in the realm to bow to it. Even the one true God's miraculous deliverance of Shadrach, Meshach, and Abed-Nego produced only a token expression of praise from the king's lips.

Nebuchadnezzar truly saw himself as an omnipotent sovereign—but God saw him quite differently. In this study, we will discover that pride does not elevate a person but debases them. In God's eyes, it lowers one to the level of a beast. However, we will also discover that the Lord sends discipline for the purpose of raising people to godliness—and that path, ironically, leads first through humility.

KEYS TO THE TEXT

Read Daniel 4:1–37, noting the key words and phrases indicated below.

THE KING'S EDICT: King Nebuchadnezzar sends out an official decree to his empire to explain a dramatic change that has taken place in his life.

4:1. NEBUCHADNEZZAR THE KING: The events in this chapter took place after Daniel's friends were saved from the fiery furnace, though it is not clear how much time had elapsed. This chapter encompasses an official edict the king sent out to the people of Babylon.

TO ALL PEOPLES, NATIONS, AND LANGUAGES: Nebuchadnezzar's edict was addressed in the same manner as his command to worship the golden image (see Daniel 3:4). This was probably a standard opening for official edicts "to all the subjects of King Nebuchadnezzar," yet it is significant that the king was going back to the same audience he had once commanded to worship an idol. This time, however, he was telling them the truth about the one true God.

PEACE BE MULTIPLIED TO YOU: Right from the beginning, we notice a startling change in the king's tone. Nebuchadnezzar had previously made a decree that "any people, nation, or language which speaks anything amiss against the God of Shadrach, Meshach, and Abed-Nego shall be cut in pieces, and their houses shall be made an ash heap" (Daniel 3:29). Now that same fiery king was opening his edict with a greeting of peace.

2. THE SIGNS AND WONDERS THAT THE MOST HIGH GOD HAS WORKED FOR ME: Here again we see a dramatic change from the king's previous understanding of God. Rather than referring to Him as "the God of Shadrach, Meshach, and Abed-Nego" (3:29), he now understood He was "the Most High God," the King of kings and Lord of lords. More significantly, the king recognized the Lord was working on the king's own behalf as well as on behalf of Daniel's friends, acknowledging "signs and wonders [have been] worked for me." Like Paul, King Nebuchadnezzar had gone from being a persecutor of God's people to one of God's people himself.

3. HIS SIGNS . . . HIS WONDERS: Nebuchadnezzar was referring to the dramatic ways in which the Lord had made Himself known to the king. God uses means both dramatic and subtle to reveal Himself, seeking to save the lost and teach all about His character. The most complete demonstration of God's nature, of course, is contained within His Word, the Bible. (The phrase should not be confused with the so-called Signs and Wonders Movement of modern times.)

ANOTHER DREAM: Once again, the king has a strange dream and calls for his magicians and counselors who, of course, fail to explain it adequately.

4. AT REST IN MY HOUSE, AND FLOURISHING IN MY PALACE: The Lord had made Nebuchadnezzar powerful and successful, but the king had not recognized the source of that prosperity. In his pride, he thought that he was somehow responsible for all of his good fortune. In this, he was like the man in Jesus' parable who thought his security lay in his possessions (see Luke 12:16–20).

7. THE MAGICIANS, THE ASTROLOGERS, THE CHALDEANS, AND THE SOOTHSAYERS: Just as before when Nebuchadnezzar had experienced a prophetic dream about a great statue, he called in his group of so-called wise men. Once again, they failed to explain the dream.

8. ACCORDING TO THE NAME OF MY GOD: That is, the god whom Nebuchadnezzar worshiped at that time, known as Bel-Merodach, an alternative form of Baal. His allegiance to that false god, however, was about to end.

9. THE SPIRIT OF THE HOLY GOD: The intended meaning here is correctly reflected in the translation, "the Spirit of the Holy God." Some believe Nebuchadnezzar meant "a spirit of the holy gods," but this is unlikely because no pagan worshipers claimed purity or holiness for their deities. In fact, they believed just the opposite. Furthermore, because Nebuchadnezzar was rehearsing his conversion, he could genuinely identify the true Spirit of God.

NO SECRET TROUBLES YOU: Nebuchadnezzar had not yet come to understand that Daniel's gift of interpretation came directly from God rather than from some innate ability he possessed.

10. A TREE: This image pictures Nebuchadnezzar after 605 BC. The king himself had compared Babylon to a spreading tree in inscriptions on buildings.

11. ITS HEIGHT REACHED TO THE HEAVENS: Here is an echo of the Tower of Babel, "a tower whose top is in the heavens" (Genesis 11:4). Human pride had led people to defy God throughout history, and that trend is still prevalent today.

13. A WATCHER, A HOLY ONE: This was an angel, a servant of God, who controlled a nation's rise or fall. Angels often have roles administering God's judgment, as shown also in Genesis 18, Isaiah 37, and Revelation 16.

14. LET THE BEASTS GET OUT FROM UNDER IT: Nebuchadnezzar had refused to acknowledge God as the source of his authority, so the Lord would remove him from his kingship. The beasts and birds in the dream represented the many peoples who were under the king's leadership. They would soon be taken out from under his dominion.

15. LEAVE THE STUMP AND ROOTS IN THE EARTH: The tree, as Daniel was about to explain, represented Nebuchadnezzar himself who had grown grand and proud in his kingly glory. The Lord was about to humble him in a most dramatic fashion, but He would not utterly destroy him. Fresh tree stumps generally put forth new growth if the roots are still healthy, and a new tree can grow up where an old one was cut down. The iron and bronze band seem to suggest that the Lord would firmly protect the king from being utterly removed.

LET HIM GRAZE WITH THE BEASTS ON THE GRASS OF THE EARTH: This is a strange shift from the tree metaphor to a person who would eat grass like a cow. Yet that is precisely what was about to happen to the king.

16. LET HIM BE GIVEN THE HEART OF A BEAST: This is some form of the disease called lycanthropy, in which a person thinks he is an animal and lives wildly, eating grass, having thick and unkempt nails along with shaggy

hair. When a man like Nebuchadnezzar elevates himself in his own mind, thinking that he is master of his own fate, he is actually debasing himself and making himself like a beast of the field. Paradoxically, it is a glory to man to recognize that he is completely dependent on his Creator.

Let seven times pass over him: This same term in Daniel 7:25 is used to mean "years," so there is good reason to believe it means years here as well. Nebuchadnezzar would suffer his madness for a period of seven years.

17. the Most High rules in the kingdom of men: Here we have a central principle of these studies: God is the supreme ruler over all human affairs. What's more, we are told that God's chosen ruler is characterized by humility, not by pride. The good king understands that he rules only by the grace of God, and that the One who raised up the king can also cast him down. In this sense, "the lowest of men" is the ruler who has a humble heart, turning constantly to God for guidance and wisdom.

Daniel's Interpretation: The Lord once again gives Daniel the insight to interpret correctly what the king's dream means.

19. Daniel . . . was astonished for a time: Daniel was astonished and troubled by the meaning of the dream, not by an inability to understand it. He was alarmed that the king was about to become like an ox of the field. He expressed a desire that the events that would soon transpire would be the fate of the king's enemies instead.

25. They shall drive you from men: The active voice ("they shall drive") might better be rendered in the passive voice here ("you shall be driven"). Nebuchadnezzar was being driven away not by people or angels but by God.

till you know that the Most High rules: The Lord made it clear to Nebuchadnezzar that his suffering was explicitly meant to teach him humility. The sooner he learned that lesson, the sooner his madness would pass.

27. break off your sins by being righteous: Daniel's advice to Nebuchadnezzar was to act in a godly manner by repenting of his sinful pride and learning to be merciful. We have seen that pride motivated King Nebuchadnezzar to a great degree, and his pride led him into frequent bursts of rage. Daniel respectfully begged the king to repent of those sins and allow God to show mercy by sparing him the humiliation that was coming.

30. THAT I HAVE BUILT . . . BY MY MIGHTY POWER: Here is the fundamental problem the Lord was addressing in Nebuchadnezzar's life. The king believed that his great success and power were due to his own efforts and that his grand building projects and political schemes were strictly "for the honor of my majesty." God did not figure into Nebuchadnezzar's plans simply because he had elevated himself to replace God in his thinking.

NEBUCHADNEZZAR'S MADNESS: *The Lord disciplines the king by letting him see the true nature of his own heart. In the end, however, the king is blessed.*

33. EAT GRASS LIKE OXEN: The Lord's discipline on Nebuchadnezzar was both appropriate and merciful. The king had raised himself in his own eyes to be equal with God, which is the most degrading and self-destructive thing anyone can do. So it was fitting that he should find himself going about on all fours, eating grass like an ox. Nebuchadnezzar looked on his kingdom and saw great splendor and beauty, but God looked on the king's heart and saw ugly bestial qualities, which He made visible to the eyes of others as well. Yet this degradation was not to destroy Nebuchadnezzar but to humble him and cause him to repent.

34. I, NEBUCHADNEZZAR: This chapter in Daniel begins and ends with the king speaking in the first person, while the period of his madness is described in the third person (see verses 28–33). This subtly underscores his temporary loss of humanity.

LIFTED MY EYES TO HEAVEN: This was exactly what the Lord was trying to accomplish in the king's life. Nebuchadnezzar had previously refused to look to God—looking instead on himself and his accomplishments—so the Lord caused him to become like a beast that can only look down at the grass it is eating. However, as we've already mentioned, the Lord's goal was only to turn the king's eyes toward heaven. The moment he voluntarily did so, his reason returned and the Lord lifted His hand of discipline.

PRAISED AND HONORED HIM WHO LIVES FOREVER: At last King Nebuchadnezzar came to know the Lord as his God. No longer was He "the God of Shadrach, Meshach, and Abed-Nego" (Daniel 3:29). Instead, Nebuchadnezzar could now say, "I . . . praise and extol and honor the King of heaven, all of whose works are truth, and His ways justice" (verse 37).

UNLEASHING THE TEXT

1) Why did Nebuchadnezzar tell the world about his humiliating madness? How is his tone in this chapter different from his words in previous chapters? What does this reveal about the king's conversion?

_____

_____

_____

2) What "signs and wonders" did the Lord give to King Nebuchadnezzar? Why? What work was He doing in the king's life?

_____

_____

_____

3) Why did the Lord send Nebuchadnezzar the dream of the tree? What was He trying to accomplish through that dream? How did Nebuchadnezzar respond to it?

_____

_____

_____

4) How did pride influence Nebuchadnezzar's life? How did it affect his reign as king of Babylon? How did humility change him?

_____

_____

_____

EXPLORING THE MEANING

Our security lies in God, not in our possessions or success. King Nebuchadnezzar is remembered in history for his grand building projects and the prosperity of the Babylonian Empire under his leadership. He was the most powerful man in the world in his day, able to make or break any man with a simple word of command. He had constructed a magnificent hanging garden near his palace to please his wife. He constructed a massive network of walls and fortifications surrounding Babylon, some wide enough that several chariots could pass one another along the top. His own palace occupied some fifty acres of land, and he used kiln-baked bricks on all his constructions to increase their strength and longevity. When he stood atop his palace, he looked on a magnificent city and told himself that he was lord of all he surveyed.

But he wasn't. No amount of military power could protect King Nebuchadnezzar from the sovereign hand of the Creator. What's more, no degree of glory and no brick-lined accomplishments could buy the king peace with God—only humility of spirit and obedience to His Word could accomplish that. This principle, of course, is equally true for all people, whether king or beggar. But the irony is that the king may well find it more difficult to obey than the beggar does, simply because the king has so much more of the world's trinkets. In this, Nebuchadnezzar demonstrated a weakness that is common to all men, thinking that his possessions and accomplishments could bring him lasting security.

Jesus warned of this danger in His parable of the rich fool who enjoyed prosperity and fertile land. The farmer became complacent in his wealth, anticipating that he would enjoy many years of life free from worry or care. It was a fairly common mistake on his part to think that ample wealth and prosperity could bring him peace and safety, for this is the way most of the world thinks. "But God said to him, 'Fool! This night your soul will be required of you; then whose will those things be which you have provided?'" (Luke 12:20). The Lord calls His children to place their security in Him rather than the things of this world and to focus their efforts on growing in likeness to Christ. This is what Jesus called being "rich toward God" (verse 21).

Pride debases a man, but humility lifts him up. The world looked at King Nebuchadnezzar and saw a man who had enjoyed success in every venture—a man who had reached the pinnacle of human achievement. Then one day he went insane. His subjects watched aghast as he foraged through his royal garden, shuffling about on hands and knees and eating grass like a cow. They watched as his hair and nails grew filthy and unkempt and the rain and dew fell unheeded on his skin. They must have wondered how such a great man could be so suddenly debased.

When God looked on Nebuchadnezzar, He did not see the pinnacle of humanity but a man who had degraded his soul through pride and vanity. It was not a coincidence that the Lord chose to have the king go about on all fours, for in this way God permitted the true nature of Nebuchadnezzar's pride to become evident to himself and the people around him. Pride is the sin of elevating oneself to equality with God, and the paradoxical result is that it actually moves one *away* from God rather than toward Him. Human beings are made in the image of God, so any move away from God is also a move away from our intended design—a move that makes us more like the beasts of the field.

Solomon wrote, "The fear of the LORD is to hate evil; pride and arrogance and the evil way and the perverse mouth I [the Lord] hate" (Proverbs 8:13). "When pride comes, then comes shame; but with the humble is wisdom" (11:2). "Pride goes before destruction, and a haughty spirit before a fall" (16:18). Nebuchadnezzar had to learn the lesson that "a man's pride will bring him low, but the humble in spirit will retain honor" (29:23).

Even the powerful must be humble to serve God. Imagine if the president of the United States one day got out of bed, stripped off his clothes, and wandered outside on all fours. Picture that powerful world leader wandering around the

White House lawn on hands and knees, eating grass and grunting like a wild beast. Members of opposing political parties would call for the president's immediate removal, and the world press would splash pictures and headlines on every front page and evening news report. It would be the end of that man's political career, and he would probably become a target of every comedian for generations to come.

God is not impressed by position or power. King Nebuchadnezzar was the leader of one of the most powerful empires in world history, yet before he could serve God, he had to realize that he was a sinner in need of repentance. God does not save the powerful in a different way than he saves others. For any people to be able to turn to God, they must realize that they have nothing that makes them worthy.

The author of Hebrews reminds us that "no chastening seems to be joyful for the present, but painful; nevertheless, afterward it yields the peaceable fruit of righteousness to those who have been trained by it" (Hebrews 12:11). Nebuchadnezzar's madness was certainly not pleasant while it lasted, but the result far outweighed the suffering, for the Lord brought him to an understanding of repentance. As Paul later wrote, "We know that all things work together for good to those who love God, to those who are the called according to His purpose. For whom He foreknew, He also predestined to be conformed to the image of His Son, that He might be the firstborn among many brethren" (Romans 8:28–29).

REFLECTING ON THE TEXT

5) Why did God cause Nebuchadnezzar to go mad? In what way was his ailment an appropriate form of discipline? What did the king learn from it?

_____

_____

_____

_____

6) Why did God reinstate Nebuchadnezzar as king after he humbled himself? Why did He not simply remove him from power?

_____

_____

_____

7) Where do you tend to find your security? What defines your sense of success or failure in life? What is God's perspective on these matters?

_____

_____

_____

8) Recall a time in your life when you were humiliated. What happened? How did you feel? What lessons did you learn from the experience?

_____

_____

_____

PERSONAL RESPONSE

9) Are you facing a time of discipline at present? What might the Lord be trying to teach you? How can you be an encouragement to someone else?

_____

_____

_____

10) What are some of the blessings you enjoy? List these below and then take time this week to thank God for each of them. Remind yourself that those blessings come from God and are not the result of your own efforts.

_____

_____

_____

5

THE HANDWRITING ON THE WALL
Daniel 5:1–31

DRAWING NEAR

What are some of the most outrageous ways you have witnessed that people have tried to challenge the reality and holiness of God?

_____

_____

_____

THE CONTEXT

When the events pick up again in Daniel 5, there is a new king on the throne. King Nebuchadnezzar died around 562 BC after ruling in Babylon for forty-two years. His son Evil-Merodach (meaning "servant of Merodach") took up his throne but kept it for only two years. His sister's husband (Nergal-sharezer) murdered him, and he took the throne for another brief reign until his own son succeeded him. This king was overthrown by a revolution in 556 BC, a mere six years after the end of Nebuchadnezzar's powerful reign. One of the conspirators, a man named Nabonidus, ascended the throne.

Nabonidus' background is not known, but he wrote in his inscriptions that he was of unimportant origins. He is believed to have been a worshiper of the moon god Sîn and to have neglected worship of the primary Babylonian god, Marduk. He eventually installed his son Belshazzar on the throne of Babylon as co-regent while he traveled throughout the empire to bolster its weakening authority. His efforts proved futile, however, as the empire of the Medes and Persians was growing ever more powerful under the leadership of Cyrus the Great.

In 539 BC, the Persian army besieged the Babylonian capital, ending the Babylonian Empire in one abrupt military venture. The events of Daniel 5 take place on that very day in the palace of Belshazzar, who was willfully choosing to ignore the Persian army that had gathered outside his city gates. On that fateful night, Belshazzar committed acts of blasphemy against God, and the Lord responded by sending a dramatic message.

KEYS TO THE TEXT

Read Daniel 5:1–31, noting the key words and phrases indicated below.

HANDWRITING ON THE WALL: Belshazzar has become king in Babylon, but his attitude is very different from Nebuchadnezzar's. One night he holds a great feast and blasphemes God.

1. BELSHAZZAR THE KING: As previously discussed Belshazzar (meaning "Bel protect the king") was actually a co-regent with his father, Nabonidus, who had acceded to the throne of Babylon after a revolution overthrew the descendants of Nebuchadnezzar. The events in this chapter occurred around 539 BC, roughly sixty-five years after Nebuchadnezzar's dream.

THE KING MADE A GREAT FEAST: The Medo-Persian army was holding the city under siege, and Belshazzar evidently decided to drown his sorrows in an orgy. It was to be his last deed as ruler of Babylon—and the last night of his life.

2. THE GOLD AND SILVER VESSELS: Belshazzar's celebration was evidently designed to boost morale and break the feelings of doom that surrounded the people. The "gold and silver vessels" were the sacred vessels from the temple in Jerusalem, which Nebuchadnezzar's army had plundered when Daniel was taken captive. It was a blasphemous act to use these sacred vessels from God's temple at a profane, drunken orgy.

4. PRAISED THE GODS OF GOLD AND SILVER: To add to their defiance of God, the revelers used the sacred vessels to sing praises to false gods. This exercise was again a call for their deities to deliver them for the Medo-Persian army.

5. THE FINGERS OF A MAN'S HAND APPEARED: Babylonian hands had taken the sacred vessels from God's temple and had raised those vessels in praise to false gods. Now, the hand that controls all people, and which none can restrain, would appear to respond to their defiance.

6. HIS KNEES KNOCKED AGAINST EACH OTHER: This would be an almost comical picture of a man stricken helpless with fear if not for the deeply serious nature of the king's defiance against God. Yet Belshazzar's attitude toward the things of God suggests he might have simply ignored a less dramatic method of learning God's message.

7. THE ASTROLOGERS, THE CHALDEANS, AND THE SOOTHSAYERS: Belshazzar responded to his crisis just as Nebuchadnezzar had done before him by calling on the secular "experts" in the empire. Turning to human wisdom and understanding for an explanation is the normal response of the world when confronted with something miraculous. As we saw previously, however, the wisdom of the world cannot comprehend the things of God.

THE THIRD RULER IN THE KINGDOM: As previously mentioned, Belshazzar's father was actually the king and Belshazzar was co-regent, which made him the second in command. Purple robes and golden chains were adornments of kings. The sad irony was that the kingdom was about to collapse. Such an offer of power would last for a matter of hours, and was utterly meaningless.

INTERPRETING THE WRITING: The king's wise men cannot interpret the meaning of the writing on the wall. Fortunately, the Queen Mother remembers Daniel.

8. THEY COULD NOT READ THE WRITING: Without God's help, the experts again failed. Belshazzar had clearly not learned from the experiences of King Nebuchadnezzar and was thus doomed to repeat the lesson.

10. THE QUEEN SPOKE: She was possibly a surviving wife or a daughter of Nebuchadnezzar, given that Belshazzar's wives and concubines were already present. If the latter, she was a wife of Nabonidus and the Queen Mother. She, like Nebuchadnezzar, had confidence in Daniel.

11. THERE IS A MAN IN YOUR KINGDOM: It is hard to believe this new king had forgotten Daniel, especially since Nebuchadnezzar had elevated him to such an important position. The life of Joseph bears striking similarities to that of Daniel, for he also was elevated to the right hand of Pharaoh—and subsequently forgotten by those who came after (see Exodus 1:8).

IN WHOM IS THE SPIRIT OF THE HOLY GOD: It is significant that the one thing people remembered about Daniel was that the Spirit of God dwelled within him. The queen also publicly acknowledged that Daniel's God was the one true holy God, which was quite distinct from the false gods being praised by the drunken king.

YOUR FATHER: This was probably a figurative use of the title, as Belshazzar appears to not have been related to Nebuchadnezzar. The fact that the queen repeated this twice more suggests she was either trying to flatter the king or, quite possibly, trying to alert him to the trust Nebuchadnezzar had placed in Daniel. She may well have been alarmed at the disparity between the leadership of Nebuchadnezzar and the drunken incompetence of Belshazzar.

12. AN EXCELLENT SPIRIT: This might refer to Daniel's attitude of willingness to serve, or it might simply mean that he had a high aptitude for such puzzles. But the unintended meaning is the most accurate: Daniel did indeed have an excellent Spirit directing him—the Spirit of God.

13. ONE OF THE CAPTIVES FROM JUDAH: This suggests that the successors to Nebuchadnezzar had forgotten Daniel's high position and value. He was once again viewed as merely a slave who had been captured during a time of war.

DANIEL'S INTERPRETATION: Daniel reminds the king of his predecessor's lesson in humility, and then he interprets God's message. It is not good news for Belshazzar.

16. THIRD RULER IN THE KINGDOM: Once again, the prizes Belshazzar offered would turn out to be short-lived in light of the city's conquest that very night.

17. GIVE YOUR REWARDS TO ANOTHER: Daniel's blunt response was not intended to be rude but to make it clear that he would interpret the writing out of obedience to the Lord and to the king, and not because of any promised reward. He might also have recognized how worthless those gifts would become given that Belshazzar's kingdom was at an end.

18. GOD GAVE NEBUCHADNEZZAR: Daniel began his explanation by reminding Belshazzar that his present authority was only by God's hand. What God had given, He could also take away.

19. WHOMEVER HE WISHED: The numerous repetitions of this phrase underscore the fact that Nebuchadnezzar had grown proud under the tremendous blessings God had bestowed on him. He had forgotten where his power had come from and had taken the credit himself.

21. HIS HEART WAS MADE LIKE THE BEASTS: As we saw in the previous study, King Nebuchadnezzar had gone mad for a time and went about eating grass like an ox.

THE MOST HIGH GOD RULES IN THE KINGDOM OF MEN: Nebuchadnezzar had learned the vital lesson that God is absolutely sovereign over all human affairs and that kings and kingdoms rise and fall according to His will—and not otherwise.

22. ALTHOUGH YOU KNEW ALL THIS: Although Belshazzar knew the history of King Nebuchadnezzar, including the important lessons he had learned concerning the sovereignty of God, he stubbornly refused to humble himself. He had evidently ignored God's earlier warnings, so the Lord would use another method he could not ignore. He would cause a mysterious hand to appear and write the message on the very walls of the king's palace.

23. YOU HAVE PRAISED THE GODS: Belshazzar went beyond refusing to humble himself before God by committing an open act of defiance against Him: using the sacred vessels to honor false gods, worshiping created things rather than the Creator. By doing so, he defied the God who had created him and placed him in authority over Babylon, and that same God was about to take back what He had given.

25. MENE, MENE, TEKEL, UPHARSIN: *Mene* means counted or appointed, and is doubled for stronger emphasis. *Tekel* means weighed or assessed, by the God who weighs actions. "The LORD is the God of knowledge; and by Him actions are weighed" (1 Samuel 2:3). *Peres* denotes divided—that is, to the Medes and Persians. *Pharsin* is the plural of *peres*, possibly emphasizing the parts in the division. The *U* prefix on *pharsin* has the idea of the English word *and*. Taken together, the phrase translates to mean "numbered, numbered, weighed, divided," as Daniel's interpretation showed. The Lord had weighed Belshazzar's spirit and found it wanting in humility before Him.

PROPHECY FULFILLED: The fulfillment to God's judgment against Belshazzar comes quickly, for in just a few hours his kingdom falls to Darius the Mede.

30. THAT VERY NIGHT. One ancient account alleges that Persia's General Ugbaru had troops dig a trench to divert and, thus, lower the waters of the Euphrates River. Because the river flowed through the city of Babylon, the lowered water enabled the besiegers to unexpectedly invade via the waterway under the thick walls and reach the palace before the residents were aware. The end came quickly, as the guards, Belshazzar, and others were killed on October 16, 539 BC.

31. DARIUS THE MEDE: History mentions no specific man with this name, so it is possible that *Darius* is an honored title for *Cyrus*, who along with his army entered Babylon on October 29, 539 BC. The name is used in inscriptions for at least five different Persian rulers. A less likely possibility is that *Darius* is a second name for *Gubaru* (or *Gobryas*), who was Cyrus's appointed king to head up the Babylonian sector of his empire. Gubaru was distinct from Ugbaru, the general, who died soon after conquering Babylon.

RECEIVED THE KINGDOM: As previously prophesied by the prophets Isaiah, Jeremiah, and Habakkuk, Babylon ultimately met God's judgment (see Isaiah 13; 47; Jeremiah 50; 51; Habakkuk 2:5–19).

UNLEASHING THE TEXT

1) Why would King Belshazzar throw a great feast when the Persian army was surrounding the city? What does this reveal about his kingship?

---

2) Why did Belshazzar use the sacred vessels from God's temple? What did this act reveal about his attitude toward God?

_____

_____

_____

3) What reasons might God have had to send His message via a mysterious hand writing on the wall? Why not just send a prophet to deliver the message?

_____

_____

_____

4) What did God's message mean to Belshazzar? What was Belshazzar's response? What did his response reveal about the state of his heart before God?

_____

_____

_____

Exploring the Meaning

God gives His people the words to speak at the right time. As we have seen throughout this study, Daniel found himself in difficult situations on numerous occasions. He was called before several kings to interpret messages from God that no one else in the kingdom could comprehend—and at times his life was on the line. The Lord had given him the gift of interpreting dreams and prophecies, and Daniel made it abundantly clear that the messages were from the Lord and that they did not come through his own strength, wisdom, or abilities. God was faithful in each instance to give Daniel the words he was to speak.

It is important to recognize, however, that Daniel did not know what he would say until the time came for him to speak. Just as he had not known the content of Nebuchadnezzar's dream until the Lord revealed it to him, he did not know what words were written on the wall in Belshazzar's banquet hall until he arrived there. We can easily imagine how unnerving it must have been for him to have no idea what to say to a king who demanded an interpretation—especially given that all the other wise men had failed. Yet this was precisely what the Lord called His servant to do. This forced Daniel to trust in God's faithfulness and sovereignty and made it clear to the king and his court that the words were from Him.

Peter urged his readers to "always be ready to give a defense to everyone who asks you a reason for the hope that is in you" (1 Peter 3:15). Christians should always be prepared to give a clear account of their testimony to others. Yet Jesus also warned His disciples that they would sometimes "be brought before governors and kings" to give testimony to the gospel. At such times, the Lord said, "Do not worry about how or what you should speak. For it will be given to you in that hour what you should speak; for it is not you who speak, but the Spirit of your Father who speaks in you" (Matthew 10:18–20). This is not an excuse for a haphazard testimony but rather a comfort during persecution. Just as God was faithful to give Daniel the right words, He will do the same for us. We can have confidence that God will enable us to be a faithful witness no matter the situation in which we find ourselves.

Worship the Creator, not His creation. King Belshazzar threw a drunken party for his friends and courtiers, and in their licentious frenzy they ate and drank from sacred vessels that had been dedicated to the Lord's temple in Jerusalem. This blasphemous act demonstrated an utter contempt for the God of Israel, but the revelers took their blasphemy one step further. "You and your lords, your wives and your concubines, have drunk wine from them. And you have praised the gods of silver and gold, bronze and iron, wood and stone" (Daniel 5:23). In doing so, they worshiped the creation rather than the Creator.

Such paganism is still practiced today—in fact, it is becoming quite widespread in Western nations. For example, many people today deny that God created the earth and humankind while simultaneously elevating His creation in His place. It is a bitter irony to treat the things of God with disdain, as Belshazzar did, while praising the very things He made. The Bible warns this idolatrous attitude will inevitably lead to the downfall of a nation, just as it did in Babylon during the time of King Belshazzar.

Paul wrote that the wonders of creation are intended to teach men about God, not to replace Him as their Lord. When a nation replaces the Creator with the creation, all forms of wickedness inevitably follow. "Professing to be wise," Paul warned, "they became fools, and changed the glory of the incorruptible God into an image made like corruptible man—and birds and four-footed animals and creeping things. Therefore God also gave them up to uncleanness, in the lusts of their hearts, to dishonor their bodies among themselves, who exchanged the truth of God for the lie, and worshiped and served the creature rather than the Creator, who is blessed forever" (Romans 1:22–25).

All earthly authority comes directly from God. King Belshazzar ruled over what had been one of the world's wealthiest and most powerful nations. During his leadership the empire of Babylon was in decline, yet his heart was still filled with pride and self-congratulation, and he took the credit for the power he wielded. His predecessor, King Nebuchadnezzar, had faced the same lesson, but he had ultimately learned what Belshazzar rejected: God gives all authority, and He can take it away as easily as He gives it.

Daniel tried to explain this principle to Belshazzar, stating emphatically, "O king, the Most High God gave Nebuchadnezzar your father a kingdom and majesty, glory and honor" (Daniel 5:18). The truth was that Belshazzar already knew these things, yet he persistently refused to humble himself before the Almighty God. Indeed, as we have seen, his stubborn pride led him to openly defy God's authority, and in the end both his kingly authority and his very life came to an abrupt end.

Most of us will never become kings or queens, yet we all interact with earthly authority throughout our lives. We exercise authority in the home or workplace, and we are simultaneously called to submit to others who are in authority over us. Recognizing that God is the source of all authority helps us remain humble in exercising what authority we have been given. It also enables us to submit willingly, even when doing so seems unpleasant.

REFLECTING ON THE TEXT

5) What does it mean that Belshazzar and his guests "praised the gods of gold and silver, bronze and iron, wood and stone" (Daniel 5:4)? How is this done in the world today?

_____

_____

_____

_____

6) How did Daniel know the meaning of the mysterious message on Belshazzar's wall? When did he receive the interpretation? What principle does this illustrate?

_____

_____

_____

_____

7) In what ways did Belshazzar fail to learn from the experiences of Nebuchadnezzar? What lessons might he have learned? How might his life have been different?

_____

_____

_____

_____

8) How did the Queen Mother differ from Belshazzar? Why did she keep mentioning "our father the king" (referring to Nebuchadnezzar)?

_____

_____

_____

_____

PERSONAL RESPONSE

9) How do you respond to authority? How do you handle the areas of authority that you've been given? How does this chapter in Daniel reflect on both aspects of authority?

_____

_____

_____

_____

10) When have you faced a situation where you didn't know what to say? How did the Lord give you wisdom and guidance in that situation?

_____

_____

_____

_____

6

DANIEL'S STAND FOR GOD
Daniel 6:1–28

DRAWING NEAR

What are some of the ways that people today try to discredit their rivals? Why do these tactics often prove to be quite effective?

_____

_____

_____

THE CONTEXT

After Daniel was transported from Judah to Babylon as a young man, he spent his entire adult life serving as a high-ranking official for pagan kings. He first served with distinction under the Babylonian kings—Nebuchadnezzar through Belshazzar—and then served as God's spokesman in the court of the Persian kings. As we saw in the previous study, this empire had risen to overthrow the Babylonians, which took place in 539 BC.

Although Daniel's career was certainly not without its difficult and dangerous times, he was generally a favorite of those whom he served. Daniel possessed experience, wisdom, a sense of history, leadership, ability, a sterling reputation, remarkable people skills, a positive attitude, and the benefit of revelation from the God of heaven. Given this, it is not surprising that his excellence at godliness sometimes raised the ire of the godless people around him.

In this study, we will see Daniel face a situation similar to that of his friends Shadrach, Meshach, and Abed-Nego, when they were confronted with the choice of bowing before an idol or being thrown into a fiery furnace. In this case, however, the circumstances are personal, for individuals in the king's court purposefully engineered the king's edict to bring harm to Daniel. Like his friends, he could have avoided the danger with a small compromise—by simply being more secretive about his faith and not openly praying to the Lord.

We will discover, however, that Daniel was not ashamed of his faith and not afraid to let others see it. In short, he demonstrated the evangelistic potential of a godly and uncompromising life. His boldness meant that he would have to face the death penalty, but in the end his testimony would have an impact on the entire Persian Empire.

KEYS TO THE TEXT

Read Daniel 6:1–28, noting the key words and phrases indicated below.

AN EXCELLENT SPIRIT: Daniel is now in his eighties, but we find him faithfully serving another king. And this king, like the others before him, recognizes Daniel's excellent spirit.

6:1. IT PLEASED DARIUS: This is "Darius the Mede"—possibly an honored title for Cyrus—who took the kingdom of Babylon away from Belshazzar.

2. THREE GOVERNORS: Darius had three men who shared the responsibilities of being second in command over the kingdom. Their primary duties were to prevent any rebellion against the king and to oversee taxes and other national financial matters. Belshazzar had named Daniel "the third ruler in the kingdom" of Babylon (Daniel 5:29), a defunct empire, but the Lord had placed him even higher in the Persian government.

3. DANIEL DISTINGUISHED HIMSELF: Daniel's lifetime of diligence and faithfulness, coupled with the Lord's faithful blessings, had caused him to excel in whatever job he was given.

AN EXCELLENT SPIRIT WAS IN HIM: This refers to Daniel's attitude, character, and his servant's heart toward both God and king. Yet we must also recognize the Spirit of God was at work in his life, giving him wisdom and blessing his work.

THE KING GAVE THOUGHT TO SETTING HIM OVER THE WHOLE REALM: Pharaoh had done this for Joseph (see Genesis 41), but the process for Daniel would prove to be different.

> *LOOKING FOR TROUBLE: The other governors and their*
> *subordinates become jealous of Daniel's favored status with the*
> *king, and they diligently look for a way to remove him.*

4. SOUGHT TO FIND SOME CHARGE AGAINST DANIEL: It is important to recognize that Daniel's enemies were the most powerful men in the kingdom, second only to the king himself. Daniel was completely outnumbered as two of the three governors turned against him. They were motivated by pure envy and jealous of Daniel's possible promotion above them.

THEY COULD FIND NO CHARGE OR FAULT: However, Daniel's diligence and faithfulness made it impossible for them to find any fault in him, though they tried hard to do so. As we will discover, even this does not guarantee a godly person will never suffer injustice.

5. CONCERNING THE LAW OF HIS GOD: Here is another sad irony in the thinking of the world. Daniel's enemies could not find any wrongdoing in his life, so they concluded that his faith in God was his one weak point! The world sees faith in and obedience to God's Word as a weakness, but when a nation sets out to defy God, the end result is to outlaw righteousness.

6. THRONGED BEFORE THE KING: The Hebrew verb here literally means "to come thronging in a tumultuous manner." It suggests an unruly mob rushing on the king in loud indignation. Daniel's enemies had no legitimate grievance against him, so they made up for it in loud bluster. It is similar to the artificial outrage of people today who take offense at the Word of God and manufacture all sorts of rules concerning what is deemed politically correct in words, deeds, and beliefs.

7. ALL THE GOVERNORS OF THE KINGDOM: This was a lie, given that Daniel had not endorsed such a proposal, but it is ever the tactic of the world to claim that "everybody does it" or "all the experts agree" concerning false

teaching. And even if such claims *were* true, God's will is not determined by vote.

> *AN EVIL DECREE: Daniel's enemies persuade the king to force all the people to worship him—and in the process they make themselves God's enemies as well.*

WHOEVER PETITIONS ANY GOD OR MAN: Daniel's enemies worded the decree carefully. On the surface it did not seem to have any religious significance, but at its core lay the idea that Darius was a god. Indeed, in the edict he was portrayed as the only true God and the only one to whom any person might pray. (The notion of such supreme deity lasting only thirty days is rather ludicrous, of course, but those who succumb to the notion they are God are unlikely to quibble over details.) Another subtlety lay in the fact that no particular deity was singled out—all gods other than Darius were forbidden. Daniel's enemies were God's enemies, and they strove to outlaw His followers from worshiping Him by using the guise of neutrality and fairness.

THE DEN OF LIONS: Ancient Near Eastern kings considered lion hunting a pastime suitable for royalty, much as fox hunting was in Britain at one time. Thus, King Darius might well have had a supply of lions on hand for his own sport, perhaps even breeding them for that purpose. The den was actually a pit in the ground with a narrow opening at the top to permit food to be dropped in without the lions escaping. (There probably was another caged door leading into the pit to get the animals in and out.) Kings (and later Roman emperors) would use these captive beasts to dispose of political enemies.

8. IT CANNOT BE CHANGED: Persian laws could not be repealed once the king enacted them.

> *DANIEL'S SOLUTION: Daniel responds to the dangerous situation by going home and getting on his knees. What he prays is surprising in many ways.*

10. HE WENT HOME: Daniel's immediate reaction to the decree was to go home and pray. It is important to understand that opening his windows was his regular practice. He was not trying to flaunt his disobedience to the king's decree, but he was also not allowing the decree to change his daily prayer

habits. Daniel may have been consciously following the pattern of prayer that Solomon had set forth hundreds of years earlier (see 2 Chronicles 6:38–39) and that his father, David, had practiced before him (see Psalm 55:17).

PRAYED AND GAVE THANKS: Here is a surprising element in Daniel's prayer. We might have expected him to grieve before the Lord, much as Mordecai did after learning of Haman's plot, but Daniel gave thanks. We are not told what specifically he was thankful for, but we can safely assume that his thanks were motivated by a complete faith in God's sovereign and faithful care of His people. The Lord calls His people to be characterized by a thankful heart (see Ephesians 5:20). This does not preclude intercession for others and making requests for our own needs, however, and Daniel's prayer included supplication for the Lord's deliverance.

13. ONE OF THE CAPTIVES FROM JUDAH: Daniel had lived in Babylon for more than sixty years, yet his enemies described him in these words to degrade him in the mind of the king. In this way they planted the seed of suspicion that Daniel might be planning some form of rebellion.

14. THE KING . . . WAS GREATLY DISPLEASED WITH HIMSELF: The king had seen himself as a god, but in one swift moment saw the truth about himself—and he was ashamed. It is a strong testimony to the character of Daniel that the king recognized his value to his rule and evidently also cared for him as an individual.

16. YOUR GOD, WHOM YOU SERVE CONTINUALLY: This is a powerful statement of Daniel's faithful testimony. Everyone around Daniel knew that he served the Lord, and did so continually, and that testimony was bearing fruit—though potentially at the cost of Daniel's life.

THE DEN OF LIONS: Daniel is thrown into the lions' den, just as his friends had been thrown into a fiery furnace. Once again, God's power and faithfulness are shown forth.

17. A STONE WAS BROUGHT: The stone was laid across the opening in order to prevent anyone from rescuing Daniel from the lions, and the seals were affixed to ensure the stone was not moved. This episode in Daniel's life paints a striking picture of the resurrection of Christ, whose tomb was sealed by Pilate lest the disciples should steal His body (see Matthew 27:66). Unlike Daniel, however, Jesus did die—yet no stone could keep Him in the tomb!

18. SPENT THE NIGHT FASTING: Darius's repentance seems to have been genuine, and he may well have spent the night praying for Daniel's deliverance.

20. HAS YOUR GOD . . . BEEN ABLE TO DELIVER YOU: The king's knowledge of God's character was incomplete, but Daniel's deliverance would demonstrate conclusively that He did indeed have the power to save. Furthermore, He not only had the power but also took pleasure in caring for those who served Him. Daniel's faithful testimony and God's faithful character combined in this episode to teach the king that there is only one true God.

21. O KING, LIVE FOREVER: This was a standard form of addressing a king in Daniel's time, yet it was also an appropriate statement for Daniel to make. He wanted the king to gain eternal life through faith in God—the only way that such a wish could come to fulfillment.

22. I WAS FOUND INNOCENT BEFORE HIM: This is a remarkably glorious statement for Daniel to be able to make. Those of us in Christ can say the same, because God sees us through the blood of His Son. No person can ever say that he or she is innocent of sin, yet God will one day declare each Christian to be so, because Jesus paid the debt on the cross.

23. THE KING WAS EXCEEDINGLY GLAD: Darius responded to Daniel's salvation with joy and gladness. His focus evidently was on saving Daniel rather than on avenging his enemies. It brought him delight to discover the nature of God's grace.

NO INJURY WHATEVER WAS FOUND ON HIM: Just as Daniel's friends had been unharmed by fire, so Daniel was unharmed by the roaring lions. The temporal world cannot harm God's people without His permission. Daniel's faith pictured God's salvation in this situation (see Ephesians 2:8–9).

DARIUS HONORS GOD: Darius is so impressed by Daniel's miraculous rescue from the lions that he issues a proclamation in the empire that all people must honor the one true God.

24. THEM, THEIR CHILDREN, AND THEIR WIVES: Persian law held that a man's entire family shared in his guilt. The Lord had commanded the same fate to Achan and his family when he was found guilty of sin (see Joshua 7:20–26).

THE LIONS OVERPOWERED THEM: This shows the lions were in fact ferocious and hungry, lest anyone attempt to refute God's power in Daniel's salvation. Even today, skeptics attempt to refute the resurrection of Christ in similar ways, claiming that Jesus only "swooned" on the cross but did not die—yet the facts of His death and resurrection are irrefutable.

25. PEACE BE MULTIPLIED TO YOU: Nebuchadnezzar had used similar words to open his own decree of conversion to faith in the one true God (see Daniel 4:1). Again we see a king expressing peace rather than wrath after coming to understand the character of God.

26. HE IS THE LIVING GOD: Darius referred to the Lord as "the God of Daniel," rather than his own God, yet his conversion would seem to be genuine just the same. Daniel's faithful testimony played a significant role in the king's newfound faith.

UNLEASHING THE TEXT

1) Why did Daniel's peers try to find fault with him? What does this reveal about their characters? What does it reveal about their priorities?

_____

_____

_____

_____

2) Why were Daniel's enemies unable to find any fault with him? What sorts of things might they have been looking for? What does it reveal about Daniel that they found none?

_____

_____

_____

_____

3) How did Daniel's enemies come up with the idea of creating the new law? What does this show about Daniel's faith? What does it say about his public testimony?

_____

_____

_____

4) If you had been in Daniel's place, what would you have done on hearing the new law? Why did Daniel go home and pray with his windows open?

_____

_____

_____

EXPLORING THE MEANING

God's people should live above reproach. The events of Daniel 6 present a profound statement of Daniel's godly character. His political enemies were motivated by base envy and were jealous of the favor the king showed to Daniel. Those enemies were the most powerful men in the kingdom, and they set all their power and resources on finding something that Daniel had done wrong. They wanted to uncover some shortcoming, failure, or character flaw with which to spoil his reputation—but they could find nothing!

Most people would cringe if they knew an enemy was trying to discover something they had done wrong. Yet that is exactly what is happening for every believer every day of the year! The enemy of our souls is the accuser of all believers, and he works diligently, day and night, to bring accusations of sin against all who place their faith in Jesus Christ (see Revelation 12:10). The blood of Christ permanently silences the devil's accusations, for through His sacrifice we are found blameless before God. However, this does not give believers the license to indulge in sin. Quite the opposite, in fact.

The Bible calls us to live lives that are above reproach so the enemy cannot find a foothold or a source of accusation against us. The apostle Paul wrote, "Do all things without complaining and disputing, that you may become blameless and harmless, children of God without fault in the midst of a crooked and perverse generation, among whom you shine as lights in the world" (Philippians 2:14–15). Paul also instructed Titus on the qualities required of elders and deacons, but possessing those qualities should be the goal for every believer: "For a bishop must be blameless, as a steward of God, not self-willed, not quick-tempered, not given to wine, not violent, not greedy for money, but hospitable, a lover of what is good, sober-minded, just, holy, self-controlled, holding fast the faithful word as he has been taught" (Titus 1:7–9). When our lives are above reproach, we shine like beacons in a world of darkness.

There is one God, and the only way to know Him is through Jesus. Darius did not understand that there is only one true God. He was blinded by the teachings of the world and believed in some great pantheon of gods who supposedly ruled the created world. This ignorance made the king easy prey for Daniel's enemies, and they deceived him into throwing his most loyal and valuable subject into the lions' den. Indeed, it was Darius's ignorance of God that led him to believe that he was himself a part of that fictitious pantheon of so-called gods.

This principle might seem self-evident to Christians, but the fact is that the world around us is completely ignorant of it. In fact, the world hates this truth because its system is opposed to God's Word and His Son, Jesus Christ. People today tolerate virtually any religious system—except the teachings of Jesus, which insist that He is the only source of salvation. One is free to teach openly about Islam, Buddhism, Hinduism, New Age ideas, and every form of paganism, but the one thing the world will not tolerate is the truth that there is only one God and Jesus provides the only way to His presence.

Yet this truth is at the very core of Christianity. Jesus stated clearly, "I am the way, the truth, and the life. No one comes to the Father except through Me" (John 14:6). There is no room for compromise on this truth, and there is no way that any other religious teaching can be melded into it. Christianity is not compatible with any world religion because it teaches there is only one God and only one way to get to Him. As Paul reiterated, "For there is one God and one Mediator between God and men, the Man Christ Jesus, who gave Himself a ransom for all" (1 Timothy 2:5–6). Any other teaching is false.

Prayer should be the first response to trouble. Daniel was one of King Darius's most trusted counselors, and he probably had a large staff of assistants. When the king was considering the proclamation forbidding prayer to the Lord, Daniel could easily have raised a powerful protest. He might also have been aware of the real reason behind his enemies' plan to discredit him, and most men might have gone to the king to protest their innocence and expose the treachery. But Daniel did none of these things. When the king's edict was signed into law, he went home and knelt in private prayer.

The reason for this is that Daniel understood that only God could resolve the problem. He recognized that God's sovereign hand was involved in the situation, and that gave him the faith to turn it over to the Lord's control. In fact, it may well have been God's sovereignty and faithfulness that moved Daniel to give thanks (see Daniel 6:10), turning a situation of defeat into an occasion of thanksgiving. He knew the Lord was in control, and he rejoiced in the freedom of putting the outcome into His omnipotent hands.

Daniel could have succumbed to anxiety and fear, wringing his hands in consternation over his predicament. But prayer is the solution to anxiety, because it is the process of taking the anxious burden to the Lord and letting Him take control. A thankful spirit is also an important element of prayer, for it grows out of the faith that God will answer our petitions. As Paul commanded, "Be anxious for nothing, but in everything by prayer and supplication, with thanksgiving, let your requests be made known to God; and the peace of God, which surpasses all understanding, will guard your hearts and minds through Christ Jesus" (Philippians 4:6–7).

REFLECTING ON THE TEXT

5) How did Daniel's testimony influence the people around him? What effect did it have in the king's life? What effect did it have on the nation as a whole?

_____

_____

_____

6) What does it mean to live above reproach? How is this done? What are some things in life that can reproach us?

_____

_____

_____

_____

7) When have you stood up boldly for the gospel of Christ? When have you compromised to avoid confrontation? What resulted in each situation?

_____

_____

_____

_____

8) In what ways does the world reject the truth that Jesus is the only way to God? Why is this truth such an offense to the world? Why is it such an important doctrine in Christianity?

_____

_____

_____

_____

_____

PERSONAL RESPONSE

9) Have you come into a relationship with God through the salvation of Jesus Christ? If not, what is hindering you from doing so right now? If so, are you bold about your faith or ashamed of it?

_____

_____

_____

10) What are your daily prayer habits? In what ways are you depending on God each day and yearning for His presence and power? What needs to change in this regard?

_____

_____

_____

7

GOD'S SOVEREIGNTY
Daniel 7:1–28

DRAWING NEAR

What are some ways that believers in Christ can know that God is in control of everything that happens in this world? How does the Bible show that God is completely sovereign?

_____

_____

_____

THE CONTEXT

As we have seen, the first six chapters of Daniel contain numerous stories of God's miraculous provision for His servants of the Lord during the time of the exile. Included in these chapters are stories of Daniel interpreting dreams and signs for Nebuchadnezzar and Belshazzar. Beginning in Daniel 7, the style of the book shifts from a storytelling approach to a straightforward recounting of the visions and prophecies that Daniel received from the Lord.

In this study we will look at one particular dream that God sent to Daniel, which bore some similarities to the dream of Nebuchadnezzar in Daniel 2 in that it addressed the Babylonian Empire and the kingdoms to follow. However, this time the kingdoms would be represented by strange beasts rather than a huge statue. In addition, the events described would extend far into the distant future—to times that have not yet come even today.

The topic of end-times prophecy, known as eschatology, is too large to address in great detail, but this study will give us an overview of God's plans for the future. More important, we will be reminded that God is sovereign over earthly affairs and human history, that He has a plan and a future for those who put their faith in Christ, and that He will never forsake those whose names are written in the Book of Life.

KEYS TO THE TEXT

Read Daniel 7:1–28, noting the key words and phrases indicated below.

> FOUR BEASTS: *Daniel has a dream of his own that bears some similarities to the dream of King Nebuchadnezzar. However, the events in this dream go farther into the future.*

7:1. THE FIRST YEAR OF BELSHAZZAR KING OF BABYLON: Daniel experienced this dream in 553 BC, approximately fourteen years before the handwriting on the wall episode with King Belshazzar that we examined in the previous study.

2. THE GREAT SEA: This superlative refers to the Mediterranean Sea, which is much greater in size than other bodies of water in that area of the world. Here this sea is used to represent nations and peoples.

3. FOUR GREAT BEASTS: These beasts represent the named kingdoms that we saw in Nebuchadnezzar's dream in Daniel 2—Babylon, Medo-Persia, Greece, and Rome. The ancient world frequently associated the sea with evil, and the writers of Scripture used the sea to represent the realm of satanic activity (see Isaiah 27:1). Something coming up out of the sea would immediately be suspicious in the minds of ancient people.

4. LIKE A LION, AND HAD EAGLE'S WINGS: The lion is the proverbial king of beasts, while the eagle is monarch of the skies. The mixed image suggests both the power and speed of the Babylonian Empire. Statues of winged lions actually stood outside the gates of the royal palaces of Babylon. Jeremiah,

a contemporary of Daniel, similarly used both a lion and an eagle to picture Nebuchadnezzar (see Jeremiah 49:19–22).

5. A SECOND, LIKE A BEAR: The second beast is an image of Medo-Persia, which began its power as a co-rule of the Medes and Persians. The Persians soon surpassed the Medes, however, and the Medo-Persian Empire was "raised up on one side" to become the Persian Empire. The "three ribs in its mouth" represent the kingdom defeated and absorbed ("between its teeth") by the Persian Empire: Babylon, Lydia, and Egypt. Bears were thought of as voracious devourers in ancient times—ponderous and always hungry.

THEY SAID THUS TO IT: The command to "devour much flesh" was fitting for the Persian Empire, which was the largest world ruler up to its time. But more important here is the fact that we once again have an unseen Controller who is in charge of all events. He is the One who commanded Persia to expand and who commanded it to diminish.

6. LIKE A LEOPARD: The leopard represents the Greek Empire under the leadership of Alexander the Great. His conquest of the world was stunningly fast (he died at age thirty-three), which is pictured by the leopard's wings. The four heads probably represent the fact that the Greek Empire was split into four separate dominions after Alexander's death: Macedonia, Asia Minor, Syria, and Egypt. Leopards are known for their speed.

The Fourth Beast: This beast is unnatural and hideous, unlike the preceding three. It also represents something not yet fulfilled in human history.

7. DREADFUL AND TERRIBLE, EXCEEDINGLY STRONG: The fourth beast probably represents the Roman Empire. But notice the emphasis on its fearful aspect, which is underscored more emphatically than the previous three beasts. That this empire is not compared to any literal animal furthers this element of dread. Its huge iron teeth and nails of bronze, which crush and rend and break in pieces, and its habit of trampling into the dust whatever it does not eat outright, suggest a wanton destructiveness. This kingdom was (and will be) characterized by brutality and lack of grace or beauty, something unnatural and contrary to the created order.

8. ANOTHER HORN, A LITTLE ONE: Horns are used frequently in the prophetic Scriptures to represent world leaders. This little horn represents the rise of the Antichrist, a human being who will speak boastfully and blasphemously.

9. THRONES WERE PUT IN PLACE: Daniel now sees heaven preparing for the Day of Judgment. The Ancient of Days is the almighty God, seated in His holiness on His throne of judgment, whose fiery wheels will consume the devil and his followers. The images of fire, emphasized with the phrase "fiery flame," represent the all-consuming wrath of God that will one day burn away all sin and wickedness from the face of the earth.

10. TEN THOUSAND TIMES TEN THOUSAND STOOD BEFORE HIM: Every human who has ever lived will one day stand before God. Some will appear before His judgment seat, and some before the throne of grace. Where one stands after this life will be determined by how one responds to God in this life.

11. THE BEAST WAS SLAIN: The beast here refers to the fourth empire (probably Rome in its modern permutation), but also to the Antichrist, whose blasphemies will be permitted for a season. His final destruction, which will occur at Christ's second coming, was also pictured by the stone in Nebuchadnezzar's dream that smashed the feet of clay.

12. THE REST OF THE BEASTS: That is, the three beasts that represented earlier empires. Their "lives were prolonged" in the sense that each empire was absorbed into its successor rather than utterly destroyed. As the Second Advent of Christ draws near, the modern descendants of all three empires will be part of the final phase of the Roman Empire, the fourth beast. Ultimately, however, all human government will be replaced by Christ's eternal kingdom.

THE SON OF MAN: Daniel's dream is not all fear and horror, for it culminates in the final triumph of Jesus Christ. But this triumph will include some suffering for the saints.

13. ONE LIKE THE SON OF MAN: This is Jesus, the Messiah, who often referred to Himself as "the Son of Man" (see Matthew 16:27). He comes with "the clouds of heaven" (Mark 14:62) and will one day return to earth in bodily form to establish His kingdom (see Revelation 20–22).

14. DOMINION AND GLORY AND A KINGDOM: Jesus Christ is King of kings and Lord of lords, the eternal ruler of heaven and earth, and God the Father has given all authority to Him. Peoples, nations, and languages are earthly distinctions, which indicate that Christ will set up an earthly kingdom for a time that will merge with His eternal kingdom.

17. FOUR KINGS: This probably refers to the most notable ruler of each of the successive kingdoms: Nebuchadnezzar (Babylon), Cyrus (Persia), Alexander the Great (Greece), and the "little horn," or Antichrist. Anything that arises "out of the earth" is earthly and therefore corrupt and subject to death. The earth groans in longing for a kingdom that descends from heaven, which will be holy and righteous and eternal. That kingdom is coming!

18. THE SAINTS OF THE MOST HIGH: These are the people who have been redeemed by Christ—that is, born-again Christians and God-fearing believers from all ages.

21. THE SAME HORN WAS MAKING WAR AGAINST THE SAINTS: God will permit the Antichrist to wage a great war against the saints, and he will even be allowed to prevail—for a season. But his wickedness will only further God's sovereign purposes.

22. THE TIME CAME FOR THE SAINTS TO POSSESS THE KINGDOM: Believers will enter the kingdom of Christ in its earthly phase following Jesus' second coming, and that life will continue forever into the eternal state.

23. DEVOUR THE WHOLE EARTH: The fourth and final human kingdom will be a worldwide order. The Lord showed Daniel that a unified world government will one day rule the earth (briefly), but it will actually "trample it and break it in pieces."

25. INTEND TO CHANGE TIMES AND LAW: The implications of this are not yet clear, but we have seen instances in these studies where kings have attempted to change God's law concerning worship. The rule of the Antichrist will include laws prohibiting worship of God and forcing worship of himself, making Darius's thirty-day prayer prohibition seem tame by comparison.

THE SAINTS SHALL BE GIVEN INTO HIS HAND: God will permit the Antichrist to persecute His saints for a time—but He will still hold absolute sovereignty over their affairs.

A TIME AND TIMES AND HALF A TIME: This refers to three and a half years, the last half of the Antichrist's seven-year rule, continuing on to Christ's second coming.

26. THEY SHALL TAKE AWAY HIS DOMINION: The final rule of the Antichrist will ultimately be no different from any other human kingdom in the sense that God will permit its authority for a time and then revoke it. No power on earth or in heaven can stand against God's sovereign will.

27. HIS KINGDOM IS AN EVERLASTING KINGDOM: God's kingdom is entirely different from any earthly government, and it shall stand firm forever without end. What is more, all those redeemed by the blood of Christ shall participate in its rule!

GOING DEEPER

Read Revelation 13:1–18, noting the key words and phrases indicated below.

THE VISIONS OF THE APOSTLE JOHN: We now move forward approximately 600 years to the time following Jesus' resurrection. John's visions, however, carry us far into the future.

13:1. A BEAST RISING UP OUT OF THE SEA: Here again we have the image of a beast rising from the sea, just as in Daniel's vision.

2. LEOPARD . . . BEAR . . . LION: Here we have the three beasts of Daniel's vision in reverse order. The leopard represents Greece, the bear is Medo-Persia, and the lion is Babylon. This time, however, the traits of those animals are combined into one beast, which suggests this beast possesses the wicked elements of all human empires. Yet this beast represents more than generic tyranny; it represents one specific human being. This man will be the final earthly dictator, and he will be opposed to the things of God.

THE DRAGON GAVE HIM HIS POWER: Daniel's vision frequently reiterated the fact that God gave power and authority to human governments, but this beast derives his power from the evil one. However, this does not remove God from the picture, for the devil can only empower the Antichrist because God allows him to do so.

3. HIS DEADLY WOUND WAS HEALED: This might refer to one of the kingdoms being destroyed, and then revived, such as the Roman Empire. But more likely it foretells a fake death and resurrection hoax perpetrated by the Antichrist as part of his lying deception. In such a hoax, the evil one would be attempting to mimic the death and resurrection of Christ, setting himself on a par with the Son of God.

THE WORLD IS DECEIVED: The Antichrist and his false prophet will deceive the whole world into worshiping Satan. Those who refuse will suffer for it.

ALL THE WORLD MARVELED: The world will be astounded and fascinated when the Antichrist appears to rise from the dead. His charisma, brilliance, and attractive (though false) powers will cause the world to follow him unquestioningly.

5. HE WAS GIVEN: The Lord will establish the limits within which the Antichrist will be allowed to speak and operate. God will allow him to utter his blasphemies and deceive the world for three and a half years. At the end of that time, the sovereign Lord will cast Satan and his minions into hell—and the devil will be powerless to resist.

7. MAKE WAR WITH THE SAINTS: Note this verse begins with the all-important clause "it was granted to him." God's saints will be persecuted and martyred during the time of the great tribulation, but *God is still in control!*

8. THE BOOK OF LIFE: This represents the names of every human being whom God has chosen to receive His free gift of salvation. This eternal aspect of salvation demonstrates that nothing—not even Satan—can ever remove one's name from the Book of Life. "All who dwell on the earth" whose names are *not* written in that book will worship the Antichrist.

11. ANOTHER BEAST: This is the final false prophet who promotes the Antichrist's power and convinces the world to worship him as God. The Antichrist will be primarily a political and military leader, but the false prophet will be a religious leader.

TWO HORNS LIKE A LAMB AND SPOKE LIKE A DRAGON: Like the Antichrist, the false prophet will put on an outward show of being godly, perhaps also claiming to be "a Christ." But his words will give away the lie, as he will speak on behalf of Satan.

13. PERFORMS GREAT SIGNS: The false prophet will perform counterfeit miracles in an attempt to claim equal authority with Christ. Elijah had called down fire from heaven to consume Baal's false prophets (see 1 Kings 18), and God will send two prophets during the end times to do the same (see Revelation 11:3–5). God warned His people that they were to pay attention to a prophet's words more than to his signs and wonders. If he urged people to worship other gods, he was false regardless of his apparent power (see Deuteronomy 13:1–5).

14. AN IMAGE TO THE BEAST: Like Nebuchadnezzar, the Antichrist will set up an image to himself, and the false prophet will persuade the world to bow in worship to it.

15. GIVE BREATH TO THE IMAGE OF THE BEAST: Notice the false prophet will give *breath* to the image, not *life*. The Antichrist will make his image appear to be alive through deceptive means.

16. A MARK ON THEIR RIGHT HAND OR ON THEIR FOREHEADS: Tattoos were used in ancient times to mark slaves and members of religious cults. The Antichrist will similarly mark his followers in some manner, and no one will be permitted to buy or sell without it—making life nearly impossible for those who refuse to worship the devil's henchman.

18. HIS NUMBER IS 666: This is the number of a man. The number 6 falls one short of God's perfect number 7, and thus represents human imperfection. The threefold repetition of 6 underscores the fact that the Antichrist, for all his power and apparent glory, will still be merely a man. The full meaning of this number and name is not yet apparent, but it will also be revealed in that day. "Let him who has understanding" be alert as that day draws near. God's people must be watchful for these signs, for the day of His appearing is close at hand.

UNLEASHING THE TEXT

1) Why do you think these prophecies were revealed through visions of animals rather than direct and straightforward revelation? What emotional response does hearing about the animals create?

_____

_____

_____

_____

_____

2) How would you describe the empire represented by Daniel's fourth beast? What characterized that empire in the past? What will characterize it in the future?

_____

_____

_____

_____

3) Which of the prophecies have been fulfilled? Which have yet to be fulfilled?

_____

_____

_____

_____

4) How can a person distinguish between true prophecy and false prophecy?

_____

_____

_____

_____

EXPLORING THE MEANING

God is in complete control over the events of human history. Throughout these studies, we have seen that God is sovereign over the affairs of this world, from the smallest details to the most dramatic miracles. He caused a king to have insomnia one night and kept three men unscathed inside the hottest furnace imaginable. He created all things with a word and caused a virgin to give birth. His Son took on human flesh while still retaining His full godhood and then rose from the dead. Nothing is beyond His power, and all things work according to His plan.

Yet we must not overlook the real-life circumstances through which He works out that plan. Some men faced death, going all the way inside that furnace or into that pit of lions. Others faced hardship of every description, with no guarantee they would live through the day. We have seen empires rise and fall, and kings and queens come and go. What's more, the future holds more of the same—and worse. We will see a worldwide empire rise to power that will outdo all other human governments for wickedness and abomination, and God's people will be called on to suffer and be martyred.

People have a tendency to see life through temporal eyes, focusing on the present hardship and dangers while missing the eternal glory that is to come. But God sees the struggles His people face—and sees far beyond them to the miraculous plans He is unfolding. God's sovereign plan was for the good of Daniel and his friends, and His plan is for good in our lives as well. He was sovereign at creation, sovereign throughout history, and sovereign over the future, He will remain sovereign for all eternity.

Every person will one day stand before God. John wrote, "Then I saw a great white throne and Him who sat on it, from whose face the earth and the heaven fled away. And there was found no place for them. And I saw the dead, small and great, standing before God, and books were opened. And another book was opened, which is the Book of Life. And the dead were judged according to their works, by the things which were written in the books. . . . And anyone not found written in the Book of Life was cast into the lake of fire" (Revelation 20:11–12, 15).

A day of judgment is coming, and every human who has ever lived shall stand before God. However, *not all will stand before God's great white throne of judgment.* The verses above describe the horrible throne of God's wrath, when those whose names are not written in the Book of Life shall be cast into the eternal lake of fire. Notice these verses reiterate "the dead were judged according to their works." This not a good thing, though the world might think so. To be judged according to one's works is to automatically face judgment, for without the saving grace of God, purchased by the blood of the Lamb, no person can gain the gift of eternal life.

There is only one way to escape the final judgment of God, and that is by having one's name written in the Book of Life. If you have repented of your sins and given your life to Jesus, your name is written in that book—and it can never be erased! But if you have not received God's gift of forgiveness, *available only through His Son,* you are at the most grave risk imaginable. The return of Christ is imminent, and the threat of judgment is real. But salvation is available to anyone who turns to God in faith. You have only hell to lose, but heaven to gain.

The devil deceives people away from God's truth. A day is coming when a man will arise and deceive the world. He will persuade every nation on earth that he is God. He will fake his own death and resurrection and will perform phony miracles that seem so real they fool everybody. His powers of deception will be so great that the world will worship him as God. His number will be branded on all people on earth, indicating their allegiance to the Antichrist.

But this work of deception is not restricted to the end times or the great tribulation. It is going on now and has been since the beginning of the human race. Satan has been a liar and a murderer since the beginning (see John 8:44). He has worked throughout human history to deceive people away from God's truth and bring souls into eternal condemnation. His great objective is to turn people away from the truth of Jesus Christ. He doesn't care who or what a person worships, so long as it is not Jesus. "Who is a liar," warns John, "but he who denies that Jesus is the Christ? He is antichrist who denies the Father and the Son" (1 John 2:22).

The devil is crafty, and his deceptions can seem convincing. But there is one way to discern truth from lies: anyone who denies Jesus is the only source of salvation is speaking a lie. John addressed this when he wrote, "By this you know the Spirit of God: Every spirit that confesses that Jesus Christ has come in the flesh is of God, and every spirit that does not confess that Jesus Christ has come in the flesh is not of God. And this is the spirit of the Antichrist, which you have heard was coming, and is now already in the world" (1 John 4:2–3). Those who reject Jesus reject the truth, and those who by default reject truth embrace a lie.

REFLECTING ON THE TEXT

5) How will the Antichrist be recognized? What will he be like? What will it be like for those under his earthly authority?

_____

_____

_____

_____

6) What trends do you see in earthly kingdoms as described in these visions? How does this compare with modern beliefs that humankind is evolving into something better?

_____

_____

_____

_____

7) What events or trends in the world today indicate the Lord's return is imminent? How does this imminence influence your life today?

_____

_____

_____

_____

8) What lies and deceptions is the devil using in the world today? How does he work to draw people away from the truth of Jesus Christ?

_____

_____

_____

_____

PERSONAL RESPONSE

9) What evidence of God's sovereignty do you find in these chapters? How does His sovereignty influence your views of the future?

_____

_____

_____

_____

10. Do you trust the Lord of history with your own life? What do you learn from these passages of Scripture that prompt you to trust your life to Jesus today?

_____

_____

_____

_____

8

A QUEEN DEPOSED
Esther 1:1–22

DRAWING NEAR

What are some characteristics of a godly marriage? What roles do wives and husbands have in such a relationship?

_____

_____

_____

THE CONTEXT

We now move forward in time some sixty years after the fall of Babylon at the hands of Cyrus the Great. During the reign of this Persian king, the empire expanded and ultimately conquered most of southwest Asia and much of central Asia. Cyrus died in battle in 530 BC and left the empire to his son Cambyses, who conquered Egypt, Nubia, and other territories. Upon his death in 522 BC the empire passed to his younger brother Bardiya and then to a man who would be known as Darius the Great, who ruled from 521–486 BC.

Darius's son was a man named Ahasuerus, who is better known to us today as Xerxes. In 481 BC, Ahasuerus led his Persian forces in an invasion of Greece, hoping to increase his great empire. That campaign failed miserably, but its execution required a great deal of advance planning. Our study opens two years before that battle with a gathering of the king's nobles from all areas of his empire at his winter palace in Susa. At this point in history, some Jews had returned to Jerusalem and started rebuilding the temple, but many were still living in exile.

The gathering in Susa might well have been the planning session for the Greek invasion. It was a prolonged time of feasting and celebration that lasted a total of 180 days. However, the events that concern us occurred at the end of that time, when the king hosted another banquet that lasted seven days. During the course of that feast, the king sent for his queen—hardly a dramatic moment on the surface. Yet his reason for wanting her and his forceful tone made the queen uncomfortable, and she refused to appear. Suddenly, a fairly common-place event turned into a highly charged political confrontation, as the queen of Persia openly defied her king. The implications quickly became profound.

In this study, we will gain some behind-the-scenes insight into the royal relationship between the king and queen, and we will have the opportunity to assess the complementary roles God has made for men and women. In the process, we will learn that our actions matter to those around us and that god-liness calls us to sobriety and humility.

KEYS TO THE TEXT

Read Esther 1:1–22, noting the key words and phrases indicated below.

A ROYAL FEAST: King Ahasuerus holds a banquet that lasts seven days. He invites everyone to attend, from the greatest to the least in his kingdom.

1:1. IN THE DAYS OF AHASUERUS: The events in this opening chapter of Esther occurred during the reign of King Ahasuerus of Persia (whose name means "prince, head, or chief") around 483 BC. The kingdom at the time was composed of twenty regions, which were further divided into provinces ruled over by governors.

FROM INDIA TO ETHIOPIA: The Persian Empire was huge by compari-son with previous world powers. Its borders extended east to the Indus River (modern-day Pakistan) and west to Greece, extending south through Egypt into Ethiopia (modern-day Sudan) and north to the Caucasus Mountains.

2. SHUSHAN THE CITADEL: The winter residence of the Persian kings, also known as Susa (modern-day Shush in Iran), was one of four capital cities in the empire. The other three included Babylon, Ecbatana, and Persepolis. The term *citadel* refers to the fortified palace complex built above the city for protection.

3. IN THE THIRD YEAR OF HIS REIGN: This probably included the planning phase for Ahasuerus's later campaign against Greece, in which the king suffered a humiliating defeat. Present at the palace were the military leaders "of Persia and Media." Cyrus the Great had inherited Media (c. 550 BC), and thus the name *Media* became just as prominent as Persia.

5. A FEAST LASTING SEVEN DAYS: Weeklong feasts were not uncommon in the ancient world. Jewish wedding celebrations, for example, generally went on for a whole week.

7. THEY SERVED DRINKS IN GOLDEN VESSELS: The setting for this feast brings to mind the drunken debauchery of King Belshazzar in Daniel 5. Of course, these golden vessels were not the sacred ones stolen from the Lord's temple in Jerusalem, but the extravagance still suggests the king's pride.

8. THE DRINKING WAS NOT COMPULSORY: Persian custom dictated that all guests at a feast were to drink whenever the king raised his cup to his lips. It is possible the king dispensed with that custom for diplomatic reasons so as to be sensitive to important members of his court who were from different cultures. It would have been important for him to build unity within his forces if this feast was in fact connected to his subsequent campaign against Greece.

9. QUEEN VASHTI: Greek literature records her name as *Amestris*. She gave birth in 483 BC to Ahasuerus's third son, Artaxerxes, who later succeeded him to the throne (see Ezra 7:1).

A DRUNKEN DEMAND: The king grows "merry with wine" and demands that his queen present herself before his friends. But the queen refuses.

10. THE HEART OF THE KING WAS MERRY WITH WINE: The Persians often drank heavily while making political decisions in the belief that drunkenness drew men closer to the gods.

11. IN ORDER TO SHOW HER BEAUTY TO THE PEOPLE: It is possible the king was hoping to inspire some sort of patriotism in his followers prior to attacking Greece, but it is at least as likely that his drunkenness had impaired his judgment. One is reminded of Herod's drunken orgy in which he made a rash promise that led to the beheading of John the Baptist (see Mark 6:14–29).

12. BUT QUEEN VASHTI REFUSED TO COME: We are not told why the queen disobeyed the king's command, but a likely reason was that she was offended at being treated like a possession for the king to brag about. Another possibility was that she was still pregnant with Artaxerxes at the time.

THE KING WAS FURIOUS: We have seen angry kings repeatedly in these studies, and we have noted that the anger of man does not work the righteousness of God. There is, however, another side to this issue. The king's command may well have been arbitrary or even degrading if he had demanded that the queen be paraded before a room of drunken men.

13. THE WISE MEN WHO UNDERSTOOD THE TIMES: These would be the same types of counselors as those who were unable to advise either Nebuchadnezzar or Belshazzar. King Ahasuerus apparently relied heavily on the advice of such worldly counselors, and his blind trust of Haman demonstrated a lack of wisdom in selecting them.

14. THE SEVEN PRINCES: These highest-ranking officials were perhaps equivalent to the "magicians and astrologers" of Daniel 1:20.

THE KING'S EDICT: *The king's counselors persuade him to make a law concerning his nation's marital relationships—which in effect ends his own.*

17. THEY WILL DESPISE THEIR HUSBANDS: Judging from subsequent events with Haman, we might be safe in assuming the counselors had ulterior motives in giving this advice. In fact, it is quite likely that they were taking advantage of the opportunity to coerce the king into divorcing his queen. Yet the larger picture is important concerning Vashti: she was the queen, and as such her actions would become an example that others might follow. If the queen could defy her husband's authority with impunity, certainly the same would apply in ordinary marriages. After all, most men do not have the authority of the king.

18. THUS THERE WILL BE EXCESSIVE CONTEMPT AND WRATH: The sad truth is that neither the king nor the queen was functioning as a moral role

model in this dispute. If women might follow the queen's example of defiance, then it is equally likely that ordinary men would imitate the king's example of rage. Paul would later write in Ephesians 5:21–33 about what a godly marriage looked like and what the responsibilities were of the husband and wife.

19. SO THAT IT WILL NOT BE ALTERED: As we saw previously, once the king passed a law, it could never be repealed. "Then these men approached the king, and said to the king, 'Know, O king, that it is the law of the Medes and Persians that no decree or statute which the king establishes may be changed'" (Daniel 6:15). This irrevocable nature of Persian law will play an important role in how the rest of the events in Esther transpire.

VASHTI SHALL COME NO MORE BEFORE KING AHASUERUS: Ironically, Vashti got exactly what she demanded—and more so. She chose to remove herself from the king's presence when summoned, and she ended up being denied access to his presence ever after.

ANOTHER WHO IS BETTER THAN SHE: This would prove to be Esther.

20. ALL WIVES WILL HONOR THEIR HUSBANDS: It is good for women to honor their husbands, but it is far better for them to do it out of obedience to God's Word rather than out of fear and compulsion. Husbands who imitate the love of Christ make it far easier for their wives to honor them.

22. HE SENT LETTERS: The efficient Persian communication network (a rapid relay by horses) played an important role in speedily publishing kingdom edicts.

GOING DEEPER

Paul would later provide instructions to Christians on the requirements of a godly marriage. Read his words in Ephesians 5:21–33, noting the key words and phrases indicated below.

> *THE ROLE OF A GODLY WIFE: Paul begins his teaching on marriage by instructing women of their roles in the marital relationship.*

5:21. SUBMITTING TO ONE ANOTHER: Paul introduces this teaching about specific relationships of authority and submission among Christians by declaring unequivocally that every spirit-filled Christian is to be humble and submissive. This is foundational to all the relationships in this section. No believer is inherently superior to any other believer. In their standing before God, they are equal in every way (Galatians 3:28).

IN THE FEAR OF GOD: Believers' continual reverence for God is the basis for their submission to other believers.

22. WIVES, SUBMIT TO YOUR OWN HUSBANDS: Having established the foundational principle of submission, Paul first applies his teaching to wives. The command is unqualified and applies to every Christian wife, regardless of how her abilities, education, knowledge of Scripture, spiritual maturity, or any other qualifications might compare to those of her husband. Submission is not the husband's to command but for the wife to willingly and lovingly offer. "Your own husbands" limits her submission to the one man God has placed over her and also gives a balancing emphasis that he belongs to her as a personal intimate possession.

AS TO THE LORD: The spiritual wife's supreme submission is to the Lord, so she lovingly submits to her husband as an act of obedience to God, who has given this command as His will for her. She does this regardless of her husband's personal worthiness or spiritual condition.

23. HUSBAND IS HEAD . . . CHRIST IS HEAD: The Spirit-filled wife recognizes that her husband's role in leadership is not only God-ordained but also a reflection of Christ's own loving, authoritative headship of the church.

SAVIOR OF THE BODY: As the Lord delivered His church from the dangers of sin, death, and hell, so the husband provides for, protects, preserves, and loves his wife, leading her to blessing as she submits to his authority.

THE ROLE OF A GODLY HUSBAND: Paul turns to instructing men of their roles in the marital relationship, calling them to love their wives as Christ loved the church.

25. LOVE YOUR WIVES: Paul addresses the supreme responsibility of husbands in regard to their wives, which is to love them with the same unreserved, selfless, and sacrificial love that Christ has for His church. Christ gave everything He had, including His own life, for the sake of His church, and that is the standard of sacrifice for a husband's love for his wife.

26. THAT HE MIGHT SANCTIFY AND CLEANSE HER: This speaks of the love that Christ has for His church. Saving grace makes believers holy by the agency of the Word of God so that the church may be a pure bride. Because divine

love seeks to completely cleanse those who are loved from every form of sin and evil, a Christian husband should not be able to bear the thought of anything sinful in the life of his wife that displeases God. His greatest desire for her should be for her to become perfectly conformed to Christ, so he leads her to purity.

28. AS THEIR OWN BODIES: Here is one of the most poignant and compelling descriptions of the oneness that should characterize Christian marriage. A Christian husband is to care for his wife with the same devotion that he naturally manifests as he cares for himself—and even more so, since his self-sacrificing love causes him to put her first.

LOVES HIS WIFE LOVES HIMSELF: A husband who loves his wife in these ways brings great blessing to himself from her and from the Lord.

29. NOURISHES AND CHERISHES: These terms express the twin responsibilities of a husband in providing for his wife's needs in order to help her grow to maturity in Christ and in providing warm and tender affection to give her comfort and security.

30. MEMBERS OF HIS BODY: The Lord provides for His church because it is so intimately and inseparably connected to Him. If He did not care for His church, He would be diminishing His own glory, which the church brings to Him by praise and obedience. In the same way, the husband's life is to be so intimately joined to the wife's that they are one.

31. FOR THIS REASON: Paul quotes from Genesis 2:24 to reinforce the idea of the divine plan for marriage that God instituted at creation. The union of marriage is intimate and unbreakable. *Joined is* a word used to express being glued or cemented together, emphasizing the permanence of the marital relationship.

UNLEASHING THE TEXT

1) How did the king's drunkenness influence the events in this chapter? How might things have been different if he had remained sober through this narrative?

_____

_____

_____

2) Why did King Ahasuerus command his wife's appearance at the feast? What reasons might she have had for refusing?

_____

_____

_____

3) If you had been in Queen Vashti's position, how would you have responded to the king's command? What other actions, if any, would you have taken?

_____

_____

_____

4) In what ways were both Ahasuerus and Vashti operating as a poor model for marriage? What did Paul say husbands and wives should do in a marital relationship?

_____

_____

_____

EXPLORING THE MEANING

Drunkenness leads to foolishness. The Persians believed that alcoholic spirits would make them more attuned to the spiritual world and give them wisdom in decisions. King Ahasuerus, however, demonstrated the foolishness of such a notion when he drank too much wine at his grand banquet. The wine did influence his decision-making ability, but not in the direction of wisdom. It is doubly ironic that he evidently recognized the dangers of drunkenness when he gave his guests the freedom to remain sober.

Drunkenness affects not only a person's physical being but also one's spirit. For example, alcohol is notorious for lowering a person's inhibitions, which is merely another way of saying that it hinders one's ability to resist temptation. And resisting temptation is a spiritual issue, not a physical concern. The New Testament frequently taught that drunkenness led a person to ignore the promptings of God's Holy Spirit and caused that person to obey the promptings of the flesh instead.

The best solution to drunkenness, therefore, is to be filled with the Spirit. As Paul commanded, "Do not be drunk with wine, in which is dissipation; but be filled with the Spirit, speaking to one another in psalms and hymns and spiritual songs, singing and making melody in your heart to the Lord, giving thanks always for all things to God the Father in the name of our Lord Jesus Christ, submitting to one another in the fear of God" (Ephesians 5:18–21). A Christian becomes the temple of God (see 1 Corinthians 3:16), and that temple should be filled with God's Holy Spirit rather than intoxicating spirits.

Provoking others leads to wrath. Queen Vashti did have legitimate reason for resenting the king's summons to his banquet. She probably felt that she was being used as a political tool or a prized possession. Furthermore, being paraded in front of a room of leering men would be degrading and offensive to any woman—and Vashti was the queen! Rather than being highly concerned with his wife's welfare and virtue, the king felt no qualms about exposing her to the eyes of strangers. No wonder the queen was not pleased with the command!

Nevertheless, the queen's response was not wise. Her husband's command certainly risked humiliating her, but that did not excuse her for publicly humiliating him in return. Furthermore, Ahasuerus was the king, which means that Vashti's defiant response was against a God-ordained authority. Proverbs rightly warns, "The wrath of a king is like the roaring of a lion; whoever provokes him to anger sins against his own life. It is honorable for a man to stop striving, since any fool can start a quarrel" (20:2–3).

Daniel and his friends demonstrated this principle when they first arrived in Babylon by gently offering an alternative to the king's command concerning forbidden foods. They were able to avoid disobeying God's commands while also not provoking the king to wrath. Paul pointed out that the root of provocation is pride—the idea that our desires are more important than someone else's. He offered a better approach: "But the fruit of the Spirit is love, joy, peace, longsuffering, kindness, goodness, faithfulness, gentleness, self-control. Against such there is no law. And those who are Christ's have crucified the flesh with its passions and desires. If we live in the Spirit, let us also walk in the Spirit. Let us not become conceited, provoking one another, envying one another" (Galatians 5:22–26).

God desires that men and women observe their God-given roles. The interactions between King Ahasuerus and Queen Vashti present a poor example of marital relations. The king commanded his wife the way a tyrant would command a lowly slave. In this way, he exercised a lordly authority in which he expected her to obey him without question. To make things worse, his command was degrading to a woman (to say nothing of a queen), for he was insisting she parade herself before strangers so they might be impressed with his good fortune.

However, modern readers should resist the temptation of forcing twenty-first-century Western sensibilities into the text. We understand that Adam was created before Eve and that Adam named her, which demonstrated his God-given authority over Eve (see Genesis 2:21–24; 1 Corinthians 11:7–12; 1 Timothy 2:11–15). We must not allow this bad example of King Ahasuerus and Queen Vashti to persuade us that the concept of male headship is no longer viable in today's world. God instituted a hierarchy of authority at the time of creation, and the principles He established then are completely applicable today. God gave Adam headship over Eve and held him responsible for her spiritual wellbeing.

There are, of course, two sides to this controversial coin, and the flip side is that God commands husbands to love their wives as Christ loved the church—which is a tall order indeed! Paul summed up these roles by saying, "Wives, submit to your own husbands, as to the Lord. For the husband is head of the wife, as also Christ is head of the church; and He is the Savior of the body. Therefore, just as the church is subject to Christ, so let the wives be to their own husbands in everything. Husbands, love your wives, just as Christ also loved the church and gave Himself for her. . . . So husbands ought to love their own wives as their own bodies; he who loves his wife loves himself. . . . Nevertheless let each of you in particular so love his own wife as himself and let the wife see that she respects her husband" (Ephesians 5:22–25, 28, 33).

REFLECTING ON THE TEXT

5) How might these events been different if the king and queen had a godly marriage? How would that compare with the king's edict to the men and women of his kingdom?

_____

_____

_____

6) What influence might the king's actions have had on the men of his kingdom? What influence might Vashti's actions have had on the women? How might their influences have been different if their actions had been godly?

_____

_____

_____

7) How did the king's brazen drunkenness influence those around him? Even though the king allowed his subjects to refrain from drinking, which were his subjects more likely to follow: his words or his actions?

_____

_____

_____

8) When have you provoked someone to anger with your words or deeds? How might things have ended differently if you had behaved differently?

_____

_____

_____

Personal Response

9) Why does God's Word teach that men are to be the spiritual authority in marriage and by extension in the church (see 1 Timothy 2:11–14)? How well are you following that model?

_____

_____

_____

10) Look back at low points of sin in your life. How was God at work during those times? What good did He bring about?

_____

_____

_____

9

GOD'S CHOSEN QUEEN
Esther 2:1–23

DRAWING NEAR

What are some the ways the world "chooses" people and determines their worth? How does this differ from the way God chooses people to be His servants?

_____

_____

_____

THE CONTEXT

King Ahasuerus of Persia had become so angry with his queen for not making an appearance at his royal banquet that he took the advice of his nobles to never again allow her into his presence. Once his wrath had abated, however, he was left with the dilemma of how to choose a new queen who would be "better than she" (Esther 1:19). Here again he listened to the counsel of his advisors, who told him to hold a beauty pageant and bring in young women to participate from all provinces of the empire.

It has been noted that the name of God does not appear even once in this book of the Bible, yet once Esther arrives on the scene, it is clear that God is orchestrating every event. In this study, we will see that God used the ousting of Queen Vashti to raise up this young Jewish girl, Esther, from obscurity to the court of the king, where she would be in position to affect the king's policies toward her people.

Another character in this study, named Mordecai, was Esther's cousin, but actually served more as Esther's adopted father. Like many of their people, they were living in a foreign land and were often faced with anti-Semitism and persecution. As we will soon see, that anti-Semitism was about to reach a peak of dreadful persecution in the Persian Empire, and God's people were about to be threatened with annihilation. The threat would catch the Jews by surprise, but not God, for He had a plan already in place.

Esther's appointment would be just the first step in God's plan for protecting His people from their enemies. Through it all, He would reveal to His people that He had not forgotten them in their exile, that He was still intimately concerned about their welfare, and that He would fulfill His promises that they would one day return to the Promised Land.

KEYS TO THE TEXT

Read Esther 2:1–23, noting the key words and phrases indicated below.

> ROYAL JOB OPENING: *The king of Persia has deposed his queen and now holds a national competition to find a suitable replacement.*

1. AFTER THESE THINGS: The events in this passage took place in approximately 479 BC—probably during the latter portion of the king's ill-fated war with Greece—and unfold over a period of approximately six years.

WHEN THE WRATH OF KING AHASUERUS SUBSIDED: The king was legally unable to restore Queen Vashti to power, so now that he had deposed her, a suitable replacement had to be found. So the king's advisors proposed a new plan with great promise.

2. LET BEAUTIFUL YOUNG VIRGINS BE SOUGHT FOR THE KING: Persian kings had the right to claim a young woman as an addition to his harem, which amounted to a collection of concubines. It was customary for such women to undergo a full year of special beauty treatments, training, and purification rites prior to becoming part of the king's harem. They enjoyed courtly

privileges and status and were housed separately from the rest of the king's household.

5. MORDECAI . . . THE SON OF KISH, A BENJAMITE: Esther's cousin Mordecai was among the fourth generation of deported Jews to Babylon. It appears that he was descended directly from Kish, the father of King Saul, of the tribe of Benjamin. As we will see in a later study, this small fact would become extremely significant in the conflict with Haman.

6. JECONIAH KING OF JUDAH: This former king, also known as Jehoiachin and Coniah, was deported to Babylon around 597 BC (see 2 Kings 24:14–15). Due to his disobedience, the Lord removed his descendants from the line of David to Christ (see Jeremiah 22:24–30).

ENTER ESTHER: One of the candidates chosen for the king's harem is a young Jewish woman named Esther. She didn't know it at the time, but the Lord has important plans for her.

8. ESTHER ALSO WAS TAKEN TO THE KING'S PALACE: We are not told Esther's views on the matter, so it is impossible to tell if she went into this forced marriage voluntarily or against her will. Regardless, she went because the king commanded it, whether she liked the arrangement or not, and in this way presents a strong contrast to Vashti. On the surface Esther and Mordecai might have viewed this as a bad situation, but the Lord's hand was guiding them, and we will soon see this was all part of His sovereign plan.

9. THE YOUNG WOMAN PLEASED HIM: Here we begin to see the Lord's invisible hand of guidance in the affairs of Esther and the Jews. The Lord granted her favor in the eyes of Hegai, the king's chief eunuch responsible for selecting the "finalists" in the contest, just as He had given Daniel favor in the eyes of Nebuchadnezzar. At the same time, Esther would not have obtained favor from Hegai if she had exhibited an unwilling or resentful attitude toward her situation. She, like Daniel, trusted that the Lord was always in control and always working in her midst, and she submitted herself under His hand.

SHE OBTAINED HIS FAVOR: It is worth noting how frequently this phrase appears concerning Esther. She found favor with all who were in authority because of God's providential control of her life, as seen through her submissive spirit.

10. MORDECAI HAD CHARGED HER NOT TO REVEAL IT: Here we have the first glimmer of foreshadowing in the book, as this suggests there

was strong anti-Semitic sentiment in the city that led Mordecai to feel safer if Esther's Jewish heritage were not known. Notice that Esther refrained from revealing she was a Jew simply because Mordecai instructed her to do so. Mordecai was her cousin—not her husband, and certainly not the *king*—yet she chose to submit to his counsel. Again, this shows her in contrast to Vashti, who defied the authority of both her husband and king. It also illustrates how dangerous it was to be a Jew in those days.

11. MORDECAI PACED IN FRONT OF THE COURT: The women's quarters would have been absolutely off-limits for any male visitor except the king and his chosen eunuchs, so Mordecai would have been unable to make direct contact with Esther. Jewish tradition holds that he was an official of some small capacity in the king's court, though later events suggest he may have held a position of some importance. Regardless, his constant concern for his cousin's safety and welfare was amply demonstrated by the fact that he made himself available to receive news on a daily basis. He did not hesitate to take the lead in his family, yet he made it easier for Esther to honor his authority by loving her in a careful and godly fashion, seeking her welfare at all times and at a cost to himself.

14. THE SECOND HOUSE: This was the king's harem—the place of the concubines.

15. SHE REQUESTED NOTHING: This is another indication that Esther held a deep respect for the wisdom of those in authority over her. Her willing submission and readiness to accept advice in turn brought her the respect of others.

16. THE MONTH OF TEBETH: The tenth month corresponding to December/January. By this time, four years had elapsed since Vashti's fall from favor.

17. THE KING LOVED ESTHER: The world would see this as mere chance—the function of the human heart alone—but in reality the Lord was fully in control. It was He who bestowed the king's favor and grace on Esther, and it was He who removed Queen Vashti and set Esther in her place. "The king's heart is in the hand of the LORD, like the rivers of water; He turns it wherever He wishes" (Proverbs 21:1).

18. HE PROCLAIMED A HOLIDAY: This probably refers to a remission of taxes and/or release from military service.

19. MORDECAI SAT WITHIN THE KING'S GATE: Once again we find Mordecai hovering nearby out of his deep concern for Esther's welfare. The author's note that the virgins were gathered "a second time" perhaps indicates the king intended to add the second best to his collection of concubines as well.

20. ESTHER OBEYED THE COMMAND OF MORDECAI: Once again, this is a striking statement. Esther was now married and no longer under the domestic authority of her cousin. Furthermore, she was now the queen of Persia! Yet she still chose to honor Mordecai for his wisdom and godliness by humbling herself and following his advice.

AN ASSASSINATION PLOT: Mordecai uncovers an assassination plot, and he saves the king's life. His reward, however, is to be forgotten, but only for a time.

21. MORDECAI SAT WITHIN THE KING'S GATE: The gate to a city was important on many levels. City officials would sit there to conduct official business and pass judgment on civil cases, much the way our modern courthouses and city halls function. Mordecai's presence in this place further indicates that he held some important position in the king's service, perhaps as a result of Esther's influence as queen.

DOORKEEPERS: These two men, Bigthan and Teresh, had become furious with King Ahasuerus, possibly over the loss of Vashti. They evidently held positions of some trust in the king's court, and they might even have been members of his personal bodyguard. They were undoubtedly in a position to assassinate the king—a fate that befell many ancient monarchs.

22. THE MATTER BECAME KNOWN TO MORDECAI: Mordecai's job at the king's gate placed him in a situation where he could easily gather information. His action of informing the king through Esther indicated a strong loyalty to those in authority over him. It would have been far easier for him to tell himself that it was none of his concern.

23. HANGED ON A GALLOWS: The Persians actually executed criminals by impalement, and it is likely they were the inventors of crucifixion. Given this, they probably impaled these men and then hanged their corpses on a gallows as a public display of what would befall any who sought the king's harm. Haman's sons would later suffer a similar fate.

IT WAS WRITTEN IN THE BOOK OF THE CHRONICLES: Mordecai's service was noted in the official records, but nothing further was done to reward him. (It is interesting that there is no indication Mordecai *expected* any reward.) Five years later, King Ahasuerus would read these Persian records during a sleepless night (see Esther 6:1–2).

GOING DEEPER

The prophet Jeremiah wrote to the Jewish exiles to remind them that God was working behind the scenes to fulfill His promise of returning them to their homeland. Read Jeremiah 29:1–32, noting the key words and phrases indicated below.

> LETTER TO THE CAPTIVES: *The prophet Jeremiah sends a letter to the Jewish captives to encourage them and remind them that the Lord has not forgotten them.*

29:1. THE WORDS OF THE LETTER: Jeremiah wrote this letter in 597 BC, shortly after the deportation of many of his countrymen, to comfort them in exile.

5. BUILD HOUSES AND DWELL IN THEM: Jeremiah's counsel to the Jews in exile—such as Esther and Mordecai—was to live as colonists and plan on being there for a long time (seventy years).

7. SEEK THE PEACE: Furthermore, the exiles were to promote peace in the city in which they found themselves and intercede in prayer for it, because their own welfare was bound with it.

11. THOUGHTS OF PEACE: This assured the people of God's intentions to bring about blessing in Israel's future.

12. YOU WILL CALL: God also gave His people in exile the opportunity to participate in what He had planned through sincere prayer. "Now this is the confidence that we have in Him, that if we ask anything according to His will, He hears us. And if we know that He hears us, whatever we ask, we know that we have the petitions that we have asked of Him" (1 John 5:14–15).

14. I WILL BE FOUND BY YOU: The Lord would answer the exiles' prayers by returning them to their land. The fulfillment of this prophecy would occur during the era of Ezra and Nehemiah, and beyond this time in even fuller measure after the Second Advent of their Messiah.

> FALSE PROPHETS: *Jeremiah now writes that the exiles must stop listening to the false prophets in their midst—for their words do not come from the one true God.*

15. BECAUSE YOU HAVE SAID: Jeremiah now addresses the Jewish captives who were rejecting God's true message and listening to the false prophets.

17. LIKE ROTTEN FIGS: The sense here is that the people had made themselves wicked and corrupt, like rotten figs, and the Lord would deal with them as such by casting them away. "Thus says the LORD, the God of Israel: 'Like these good figs, so will I acknowledge those who are carried away captive from Judah, whom I have sent out of this place for their own good.... And as the bad figs which cannot be eaten, they are so bad ... I will deliver them to trouble into all the kingdoms of the earth" (Jeremiah 24:5, 8–9).

21. AHAB ... AND ZEDEKIAH: Two false Israelite prophets who had been misleading their fellow exiles in Babylon. They would stir up the wrath of their captor king, who would cast them into a furnace (like Daniel's friends). They aroused, not only the Babylonian potentate's enmity, but also God's because they prophesied against His word and committed physical adultery.

24. SPEAK TO SHEMAIAH: The Lord's judgment against this otherwise unknown false prophet who opposed Jeremiah was to be cast out and not witness the good that God would do for his people (see verse 32).

UNLEASHING THE TEXT

1) If you had been in Esther's place, how would you have reacted when the king commanded you to become his concubine? How would you have reacted in Mordecai's place?

_____

_____

_____

_____

2) How did Esther respond to becoming part of the king's harem? How did she not respond? In what ways were her actions and attitude different from Vashti?

_____

_____

_____

_____

3) What people came to look on Esther with favor in these passages? Why? What part did Esther play in that process? What part did God play?

_____

_____

_____

_____

4) Why did Esther not request anything from the king's treasures when she had the opportunity? What did this reveal about her character?

_____

_____

_____

EXPLORING THE MEANING

God puts us where He wants us for His specific purposes. Joseph had once rocketed from a prison pit to the throne of Egypt, the most powerful nation in the world at the time. Daniel had gone from being a prisoner of war to becoming the most trusted counselor of the Babylonians, another powerful nation of its day. In the same manner, we see a young Jewish woman named Esther suddenly whisked from complete obscurity to become queen of the world's most powerful empire. It is easy, in retrospect, to see God's sovereign hand in such instances because they are so dramatic and miraculous.

Yet the same principle is always at work in the mundane day-to-day realities of our lives. Esther was indeed whisked to the throne, but before that could happen, she had to endure being wrenched from her home and family and married without having her own inclinations considered. Year after year, Mordecai worked a steady job that probably did not seem dramatic or miraculous—yet the Lord placed him exactly where he needed to be. Even Daniel had to endure a lengthy period of uncertainty and danger before he saw God's miraculous blessings.

The fact is that before God could reveal His miraculous plans for these people, they were required for a period of time to be faithful to some less-dramatic occupation. The same principle holds true for us: God has placed us exactly where He wants us to be in order to work out a bigger plan in our lives and in the lives of others. Esther and Mordecai could not see what God intended to do through them, and neither can we. Our job is to work diligently and faithfully wherever the Lord has placed us, and He will take care of the future.

Find favor in God's eyes. Daniel, Mordecai, and Esther all demonstrated an overriding characteristic: they were concerned primarily with finding favor in God's eyes. Daniel and his friends refrained from eating food sacrificed to idols simply because it had been forbidden by God's Word. Esther and Mordecai developed a lifetime habit of obeying God that enabled them to keep a godly perspective in the face of unexpected trials.

Yet in each case, these men and women were also faced with the risk of losing favor in the eyes of men—and sometimes in danger of the king's fearsome wrath as well. Daniel's refusal to eat the forbidden foods set him at odds with King Nebuchadnezzar's direct commands. His refusal to alter his habits of praying to the Lord set him at odds with the satraps and governors who were jealous of his exalted position in the Persian court. Mordecai's decision to uncover the plot against the king would have set him at odds with those opposed to the king. As we will soon discover, Esther would also face a decision that had the potential to put her at odds with the Persian king.

Yet all these individuals were willing to risk losing the favor of men because they had set a higher priority on obeying God's Word. It is no coincidence that, in the long run, they also found favor with the king, even though they had gone against the pressures of the world around them, for "when a man's ways please the LORD, He makes even his enemies to be at peace with him" (Proverbs 16:7). As Christians, our priority is always to be doing the will of the Father and striving to please Him in all our ways. James warns us, "Do you not know that friendship with the world is enmity with God? Whoever therefore wants to be a friend of the world makes himself an enemy of God" (James 4:4).

When facing a trial, remember that God is always in control. Esther must have been caught off guard (to say the least) when she was informed of her impending marriage to the king of Persia—regardless of her own desires. She must have felt the situation was a bit out of control, for she was a Jew marrying into Persian nobility. Likewise, Daniel certainly must have felt fear and sorrow as he was carried forcibly away from his home as a prisoner of war. Even Mordecai must have been grieved and fearful when his beloved cousin was led off to join the king's harem and was sequestered in quarters where no man was permitted.

In spite of this, we see that God was always in control. He was carefully manipulating the events so Esther would first be chosen from among all the other women, then find favor with Hegai, the king's eunuch, and then finally find favor with Ahasuerus himself. Esther's story reveals that we do not always know what purpose the Lord is working toward through our present time of trials. Like Esther and Mordecai—and many others who have endured trials and times of uncertainty—we must cling firmly to the knowledge that God is always in charge and is faithfully working out a plan for our blessing.

Often when life is unsteady, all we can be certain of is the one unalterable fact that relief and deliverance will arise and that God will always prove faithful to His people. It can be easy to forget this important truth when trials are raging about us, yet those are the very times when remembering this principle is the most vital. The author of Hebrews reminds us to draw near to God "with a true heart in full assurance of faith, having our hearts sprinkled from an evil conscience and our bodies washed with pure water. Let us hold fast the confession of our hope without wavering, for He who promised is faithful" (Hebrews 10:22–23).

REFLECTING ON THE TEXT

5. Why did Esther not reveal the fact that she was a Jew? When should a Christian make his or her faith known openly to others?

---

6. How did Esther show that she was respecting the Persian king's God-given authority? How did Mordecai demonstrate this through his actions?

_____

_____

_____

_____

7. In what ways can you see God's sovereign hand at work in the events of this study?

_____

_____

_____

_____

8. What purpose might God have for placing you where you are at present? What task might He have for you to fulfill? What are you doing to accomplish that task?

_____

_____

_____

_____

PERSONAL RESPONSE

9. Are you presently facing a situation in which it is hard to see God's sovereign hand? How can you deliberately remind yourself this week that He is in control?

_____

_____

_____

10. Which is generally the focus of your thinking: the opinions of others or the opinion of God? What areas of your life might need to be reassessed in light of God's opinion?

_____

_____

_____

10

A DEADLY CONSPIRACY

Esther 3:1–4:17

DRAWING NEAR

What are some conspiracies that have been launched against groups of people today? What factors allow those conspiracies to succeed?

_____

_____

_____

THE CONTEXT

During the time of Israel's exodus from Egypt, nearly 1,000 years before our study opens, the Amalekites had sent out their army to attack the people of Israel without provocation. The Lord declared at that time that He would wipe out the Amalekites from existence for their betrayal. Hundreds of years later, God commanded King Saul to carry out that sentence by exterminating the nation of Amalek, but he did not obey fully. Saul did kill most of the people, but he kept the best of their possessions for himself, and he allowed the Amalekite king, Agag, to remain alive.

In this study, we will meet a descendant of King Agag named Haman, who had been promoted to a high position of authority in the government of the Persian Empire. The king had made Haman second to himself, much as Pharaoh had done for Joseph nearly 1,500 years earlier. There was, however, a striking difference between Haman and Joseph: Haman hated the Jews. We will discover that Saul's disobedience continued to have ramifications for God's people more than 500 years later.

As we have seen, the laws of Persia made it impossible for anyone to repeal a decree from the king, so once a law was written, it remained in effect permanently. Imagine, then, how devastating it would be if a law were written making it legal—indeed, a requirement—to murder all the Jews living in the kingdom. That is precisely what happened during Queen Esther's reign, but once again God was not caught unaware. He had raised up Esther for such a time as this, and He would now call to her to take a bold step of faith for the Jews.

In this study, we will see how the ancient conflict between the descendants of Agag and the people of God came to a head. We will also learn some important aspects of a godly character, as demonstrated in the life of Mordecai, and contrasted in the character of Haman.

KEYS TO THE TEXT

Read Esther 3:1–4:17, noting the key words and phrases indicated below.

BOWING BEFORE HAMAN: After Esther becomes queen, the king orders all his subjects to pay homage to Haman. Yet there is one man in the city who refuses: Mordecai.

3:1. HAMAN . . . THE AGAGITE: We previously learned about Haman's ancestry and about King Agag and the Amalekites, whom King Saul had been commanded to kill. We have also seen that Mordecai himself was a descendant of King Saul. These events took place in 474 BC, approximately five years after Esther entered the king's household

SET HIS SEAT ABOVE ALL THE PRINCES: We are not told why King Ahasuerus honored Haman in this manner. In fact, the author may have deliberately omitted the reason in order to increase the contrast between Haman, the undeserving recipient of honor, and Mordecai, the unrecognized hero who had foiled a plot against the king.

2. MORDECAI WOULD NOT BOW OR PAY HOMAGE: God's law forbade His people to bow in worship before idols (see Exodus 20:4–6), but that might

not have been the reason for Mordecai's refusal. Ancient historians wrote that Persian court etiquette required a person to bow to his superiors as an act of respect, not worship, and the Jews themselves would sometimes bow before kings (see 1 Samuel 24:8). It seems more likely that Mordecai remembered the Lord's command concerning the Amalekites: "You will blot out the remembrance of Amalek from under heaven. You shall not forget" (Deuteronomy 25:19).

4. MORDECAI HAD TOLD THEM THAT HE WAS A JEW: It seems odd that Mordecai would not follow the advice he had given to Esther (see 2:10), but he was probably forced to reveal his Jewish identity as the reason for his refusal to bow before Haman.

5. HAMAN WAS FILLED WITH WRATH: The wrath of men is a recurring theme in these studies, and once again we see that it does not lead toward God's righteousness. Notice that Haman had the respect of nearly everyone in the empire, but he could not get over the fact that one man in the kingdom refused to bow to him.

6. HAMAN SOUGHT TO DESTROY ALL THE JEWS: Mordecai had not forgotten God's commands concerning the Amalekites, but neither had Haman. He nursed an ancient resentment toward the people of God from an event that had occurred more than 500 years earlier.

7. THEY CAST PUR (THAT IS, THE LOT): The Persians would cast lots, which they called Pur, to determine the "will of the gods" they served. This would be similar to tossing dice to make a decision. From the Persian word *Pur*, the Jews named their celebration *Purim* to commemorate the events of this book. There would have been an eleven-month interval between Haman's decree and its expected fulfillment.

HAMAN'S PLOT: *Haman's wrath has been stirred by Mordecai's refusal to bow to him, and now he uses his position to carry out his hatred against the people of God.*

8. THEIR LAWS ARE DIFFERENT . . . THEY DO NOT KEEP THE KING'S LAWS: The first part of Haman's claim against the people of Israel might have been true, for the Jews did observe laws that seemed strange to the Persians. However, the second statement was a pure lie. By mixing fact with falsehood, Haman made his scheme seem more legitimate to the king. His tactic was to couch his wicked plan in terms of protecting the king from potential rebellion. In this

way he made it appear that he was looking out for national interests rather than waging a personal vendetta.

9. THEY BE DESTROYED: Not only was Haman trying to get revenge on Mordecai, but he was also acting on an overriding hatred of the entire Jewish race. Haman was carrying out a deliberate plan of genocide based on an ancient grudge toward the people of God.

TEN THOUSAND TALENTS OF SILVER: This was a huge sum, amounting to approximately 375 tons of silver! Greek historian Herodotus wrote that the annual royal income of the Persian Empire was 15,000 talents, so this was equal to two-thirds of the national tax revenues. Haman did not intend to pay it out of his own funds but to loot it from the murdered Jews, which suggests the Jews had grown fairly prosperous during their exile in Persia.

10. SIGNET RING: The king's ring had a unique seal engraved upon it, which he would impress into hot wax on official decrees. Giving that ring to another person demonstrated absolute trust, and the king gave Haman authority equal to his own.

11. DO WITH THEM AS SEEMS GOOD TO YOU: Given the plots again the king's life, Ahasuerus would have been eager to eliminate any rebellion against his authority, though he did not seem to be interested in the money Haman was offering. However, in approving this decree, the king was unwittingly authorizing an order that would result in the death of his queen.

ANCIENT ANIMOSITY: Haman is a descendant of King Agag, last king of the Amalekites, who were destroyed by Israel. He is still motivated by that ancient grudge.

THE AGAGITE: Haman's hatred of the Jews amounted to a national prejudice that had been nursed for hundreds of years. He was continuing the animosity that had begun between the Israelites and his own forbears hundreds of years before when the Amalekites had attacked God's people (see Exodus 17:8–16, when God's people left Egypt). Ironically, his hatred was actually bringing about the fulfillment of God's promise to "utterly blot out the remembrance of Amalek from under heaven" (verse 14).

12. THE THIRTEENTH DAY OF THE FIRST MONTH: Historians have calculated this date to be April 7, 474 BC.

13. TO DESTROY, TO KILL, AND TO ANNIHILATE ALL THE JEWS: This decree mirrors the Lord's command to King Saul concerning the Amalekites:

"Now go and attack Amalek, and utterly destroy all that they have, and do not spare them" (1 Samuel 15:3). Haman was basically trying to do to the Jews what the Lord had commanded Israel to do to his ancestors.

IN ONE DAY, ON THE THIRTEENTH DAY OF THE TWELFTH MONTH: Historians have calculated this date to be March 7, 473 BC. It was an ambitious plot on Haman's part to annihilate all the Jews in just one day, but he allowed a full year for the people to prepare for their day of slaughter. This amount of time was also needed because the Persian Empire was so large that it would have taken time for the king's decree to reach its borders.

15. THE CITY OF SHUSHAN WAS PERPLEXED: *Perplexed* is actually an amusing understatement. Imagine the confusion and chaos that would ensue if a king today suddenly commanded all his subjects to wantonly murder every Jew on a certain day in the next year and loot their homes—and to do so, not only without fear of punishment, but out of obedience to the law! Even this pagan population was puzzled at the extreme and deadly racism of the king and Haman.

SACKCLOTH AND ASHES: Mordecai learns of Haman's scheme to annihilate the Jews and is filled with grief. Queen Esther, however, has not yet learned of the plot.

4:1. ALL THAT HAD HAPPENED: When Mordecai learned the king had authorized Haman's wicked decree, he tore his clothes and put on sackcloth and ashes. Sackcloth was a coarse material used in sacking that was comparable to burlap. Wearing sackcloth, tearing one's clothes, and covering one's head with ash was an outward sign of deep mourning and grief. Mordecai certainly was grieving over the wicked decree, but he might also have been feeling he had personally brought it on the Jews. But Haman's wrath had been kindled by Mordecai's obedience to God's Word, and the Lord was using these events to unfold His plan.

2. THE KING'S GATE: As we have seen, Mordecai's official position in the king's court involved sitting in the king's gate (see Esther 2:19), the place where much official business was conducted on a daily basis. A person in sackcloth would have been unseemly in such a place, like a beggar wandering into the king's court. Mordecai's open lamentations placed him at risk, as he could not carry out his duties inside the gate.

5. **WHAT AND WHY:** Esther sent Hathach, a trusted eunuch who knew of her Jewish background, to find out why Mordecai was going about in open mourning and loud lamenting about the city. Esther would quickly discover the reason.

7. **THE SUM OF MONEY:** This refers to the huge sum of money that Haman had offered the king for the privilege of exterminating the Jews. The fact that Mordecai knew of such details again indicates that he held a position of influence at the court—or it might merely demonstrate how much talk was generated by Haman's stunning plan!

8. **SHOW IT TO ESTHER AND EXPLAIN IT TO HER:** Esther had evidently not yet heard about Haman's wicked scheme against her people, probably because King Ahasuerus carefully shielded his queen and his harem from any outside influences.

THAT HE MIGHT COMMAND HER: It seems surprising that Mordecai continued to take it for granted that he could command the queen. Yet here again we see the humble spirit that Esther maintained, even in her exalted situation. She was queen over the most powerful nation on earth, but she still remained open to her cousin's guidance.

ESTHER'S DILEMMA: Esther realizes that to go before the Persian king without being summoned could result in her death. She also tells Mordecai she has not been summoned in thirty days.

11. **PUT ALL TO DEATH:** Even though Esther was the queen, she was not exempt from the king's law that anyone entering his presence without an invitation would be put to death. Furthermore, she might have feared that she had lost favor with the king, as he had not summoned her recently. Mordecai was, in effect, asking Esther to risk her very life for her people.

THE GOLDEN SCEPTER: The caveat to this law was that if the king held out his golden scepter (a sign of his kingly authority) a person could enter his presence. This practice evidently protected the king from would-be assassins, as he would only extend the scepter to those he knew and from whom he welcomed a visit.

13. **DO NOT THINK . . . THAT YOU WILL ESCAPE:** Esther had not revealed the fact that she was a Jew, and it is possible that she thought she could escape detection. If she did entertain such a notion at all, however, she quickly abandoned it.

14. RELIEF AND DELIVERANCE WILL ARISE FOR THE JEWS: Mordecai demonstrated a healthy faith in God's sovereign power to preserve His people. He confidently declared that the Lord would find a way to deliver His people from destruction—with or without the cooperation of the queen.

FOR SUCH A TIME AS THIS: Mordecai also recognized that God's sovereignty extended to all affairs of their lives. He saw that the Lord had indeed placed Esther on the throne of Persia so that she might be involved in His plan to protect His people. The flip side to this principle, however, was that Esther had to choose to obey if she were to fulfill the Lord's purpose in her own life.

16. FAST FOR ME: The text does not mention that prayer was included, such as was Daniel's practice (see Daniel 9:3), though it surely was. Esther did not pretend her task was easy, and she knew it was beyond her own power to succeed. She understood the outcome of the situation was entirely in the Lord's hands and called on her fellow Jews to join her seeking the Lord for their deliverance.

IF I PERISH, I PERISH: Here we see the true nature of Esther's heart: she was fully committed to obeying God, even if it meant sacrificing her life in the process.

UNLEASHING THE TEXT

1. In what ways did Haman deceive the king regarding the Jews? How did this happen? How might the king have ruled more wisely in this situation?

_____

_____

_____

2. What motivated Haman to try to annihilate the Jews? Where did his deep hatred come from? Was he justified for feeling that way?

_____

_____

_____

3. If you had been a Jew in Persia at this time, how would you have reacted to Haman's decree? How would you have reacted if you had been a Gentile at the time?

_____

_____

_____

4. In what ways can you see God's sovereign hand guiding the events of these passages? What does this teach about His sovereignty in the affairs of our own lives?

_____

_____

_____

_____

EXPLORING THE MEANING

Treat others the way you would like to be treated. The character of Haman provides a stark contrast to that of Esther and Mordecai. He was a man who looked out for his own interests at all times, strove to glorify himself, and worked to destroy his enemies. His hatred for the Jews, though deep seated, was sparked simply because one man in the kingdom would not bow to him. In every way he embodied the world's primary teaching: "Look out for number one."

God's Word, however, teaches a different principle: we are to regard others better than we regard ourselves. Paul wrote, "Let nothing be done through selfish ambition or conceit, but in lowliness of mind let each esteem others better than himself" (Philippians 2:3). Solomon warned against a selfish way of life when he wrote, "Whoever digs a pit will fall into it, and he who rolls a stone will have it roll back on him" (Proverbs 26:27). Haman was unwittingly setting a series of events into motion that would bring about not only his own destruction but also the destruction of his family.

The Lord Jesus Christ summed up this principle of loving others more than ourselves in what we today call the Golden Rule: "But I say to you who hear: Love your enemies, do good to those who hate you, bless those who curse you, and pray for those who spitefully use you. To him who strikes you on the one cheek, offer the other also. And from him who takes away your cloak, do not withhold your tunic either. Give to everyone who asks of you. And from him who takes away your goods do not ask them back. And just as you want men to do to you, you also do to them likewise"(Luke 6:27–31).

The Lord protects His people. Haman had been elevated to a position in the Persian Empire that made him one of the most powerful men in the world. When the king handed Haman his signet ring, he gave him the ability to write laws that could not be reversed. Whatever Haman chose to do would be put into effect throughout the Persian Empire, and there was no one who could speak against him. From a human perspective, the people of God were powerless against this man who hated them, and his decree to annihilate them spelled the end for the nation of Israel.

However, as we have seen throughout these studies, God is infinitely more powerful than any human being or nation on earth, and there is no one who can stand against His sovereign control. This is great news for us today, because God has promised to care for those who obey His Word—for those who have accepted His gift of salvation through His Son, Jesus Christ. The Holy Spirit seals us as Christians, and we each bear the image of Jesus that can never be removed. We belong to God, and He will protect us from those who seek our harm.

Paul addressed this sealing when he wrote, "Now He who establishes us with you in Christ and has anointed us is God, who also has sealed us and given us the Spirit in our hearts as a guarantee" (2 Corinthians 1:21–22). This is the guarantee of our eternal inheritance. While the Lord might call us at times to endure persecution, in the end He will never permit the enemy to do us eternal harm. "Because you have kept My command to persevere," the Lord said to the church at Philadelphia, "I also will keep you from the hour of trial which shall come upon the whole world, to test those who dwell on the earth. Behold, I am coming quickly! Hold fast what you have, that no one may take your crown" (Revelation 3:10–11).

Christians should not be surprised by persecution. This represents the flip side to the previous principle. In times of trial the Lord will protect His children from the evil one, but that does not necessarily mean we will *never* suffer persecution. God called Esther and Mordecai—and indeed, all the Jews living in Persia—to endure a time of danger and terrific threat. Although that threat was never realized, God's people in other ages have endured greater trials, being called even to face martyrdom at the hands of their enemies.

We must remember that the things of this world will come to an end—including our possessions, our welfare, and even our earthly lives. There have been times throughout history when the Lord called on His people to sacrifice those things for His sake, even to the point of shedding their own blood and losing their lives. There are Christians even today who face imprisonment and loss for the sake of the gospel, and we should not be caught by surprise if the same should happen to us. Yet as we have seen, the Lord is faithful to strengthen and guide His servants through such times, just as He guided Daniel, Mordecai, Esther, and others.

The reason for such persecution is that the world hates Christ—and if it hates Christ, it also hates those who belong to Him. As Jesus warned, "If the world hates you, you know that it hated Me before it hated you. If you were of the world, the world would love its own. Yet because you are not of the world, but I chose you out of the world, therefore the world hates you. Remember the word that I said to you, 'A servant is not greater than his master' If they persecuted Me, they will also persecute you" (John 15:18–20). We should thus consider it an honor if we suffer for being a Christian, for we are sharing in the sufferings of Christ.

REFLECTING ON THE TEXT

5) What were the long-range consequences of Saul's failure to obey God's command to completely destroy the Amalekites? What does this teach about the importance of complete obedience to God?

_____

_____

_____

6. How might this story have been different if Haman had treated others the way he liked being treated himself? How does this illustrate Jesus' commands?

_____

_____

_____

7. Why did the Lord allow His people to suffer from Haman's persecution? What does this teach about the suffering that Christians might face?

_____

_____

_____

8. When have you suffered persecution for your faith in Christ? How did you respond to it? How might you respond differently in the future?

_____

_____

_____

PERSONAL RESPONSE

9. When have you recently treated someone in a way that you would not like being treated yourself? How can you make amends?

_____

_____

_____

10. Why is it common for those in positions of power to try to muzzle or control others? In what ways have you been guilty of this? How will you change this about yourself?

_____

_____

_____

11

SALVATION FOR GOD'S PEOPLE
Esther 5:1–7:10

DRAWING NEAR

What does it mean when a person has a "comeback"? What are some of the greatest comeback stories that you have witnessed?

_____

_____

_____

THE CONTEXT

Haman had deceived King Ahasuerus into issuing a law to annihilate all the Jews in the Persian Empire. The only person who could influence the king to help prevent this genocide was Queen Esther, but to do so would require her to put her life on the line. She had not been invited into the king's presence for many days—and his willingness to impulsively replace the previous queen when she angered him made the threat very great indeed.

Fortunately, as we will see in this study, Esther possessed not only great physical beauty but also a shrewd intellect. Once the king extended the golden scepter to her—thus preserving her life—she cunningly played into Haman's pride by inviting him to a series of banquets. In this way, Esther also won the king's confidence before expressing her important request to him. For Haman the end was near—though he remained deluded almost right up to the end.

The end of Haman and the subsequent salvation of God's people demonstrate the theme we have discussed throughout this study: God is always in control of events. Although Satan had used Haman and others in the empire to bring an end to God's people—and thus eliminate the possibility of a Messiah—God used all the enemy's plans for good. As Joseph had once said to his brothers, who had likewise plotted wickedness against him, "You meant evil against me; but God meant it for good, in order to bring it about as it is this day, to save many people" (Genesis 50:20).

Keys to the Text

Read Esther 5:1–7:10, noting the key words and phrases indicated below.

FINDING FAVOR WITH THE KING: After three days of prayer and fasting, Esther puts her life on the line and enters the king's presence unbidden. His response will have profound consequences.

5:1. THE KING SAT ON HIS ROYAL THRONE: God was in control even over such small details as where the king sat and which direction he was facing the moment Esther entered the courtyard. In this situation, Esther was able to stand far off from the king and wait for him to see her.

2. SHE FOUND FAVOR IN HIS SIGHT: Esther found favor in the sight of the king because she had first found favor in the sight of God (see Proverbs 21:1).

3. IT SHALL BE GIVEN TO YOU: From a human perspective, the tables suddenly turned for Esther and the Jews when she found favor with the king. However, the truth is that the tables were never against God's people in the first place, for God had His sovereign hand on all events from before the beginning of time.

UP TO HALF THE KINGDOM: This was royal hyperbole and not intended to be taken at face value (see Mark 6:22–23).

4. THE BANQUET THAT I HAVE PREPARED: This would be the first of two banquets that Esther prepared for the king and Haman. Her invitation

to Haman ensured that he would be present when she ultimately exposed his wickedness.

> BUILD THE GALLOWS: *Haman is pleased to be invited to the banquet, but his joy quickly fades when he sees Mordecai standing in the gate. His family suggests that he have the Jew hanged.*

5:9. JOYFUL AND WITH A GLAD HEART: Haman was pleased to have been considered so important by the queen that she invited him to a series of banquets. Yet the mere sight of Mordecai refusing to "stand or tremble before him" was enough to instantly nullify his great rejoicing. This demonstrates the all-consuming hatred that Haman had toward God's people, as well as the shallowness and vanity of his character. The fact that Mordecai was back at the king's gate also indicates that he had removed the sackcloth and resumed normal clothing. This and his refusal to tremble in the presence of the one who had decreed his death demonstrate the depth of Mordecai's faith: he knew the Lord would deliver His people.

11. TOLD THEM OF HIS GREAT RICHES: Here again we are reminded of the Lord's parable of the rich fool (see Luke 12:13–21). Haman's boasting about his riches, his sons (he fathered at least ten), and his success presupposed that all these blessings had come to him through his own merit (though no merit was mentioned for his promotion in the king's service).

14. THAT MORDECAI BE HANGED ON IT: This scheme probably involved impaling Mordecai and then hanging his body for display, just as had befallen the two eunuchs (see Esther 2).

> THE WHEEL TURNS: *The king has insomnia that night and asks that the court records be read to him. He soon discovers that he has failed to honor Mordecai for foiling the earlier plot.*

6:1: THE KING COULD NOT SLEEP: On the very night that Haman was building a gallows for Mordecai, the king happened to suffer from insomnia. The solution to his problem was to have the book that chronicled an assassination attempt read to him. (That attempt had probably occurred some five years earlier.) From a human perspective this would seem to be an amazing coincidence, but God's Word reveals it was no accident—it was part of God's deliberate plan. There are no coincidences or surprises under the Lord's sovereign hand.

3. NOTHING HAS BEEN DONE FOR HIM: The world's system is often unjust, rewarding the unworthy (like Haman) while ignoring those who deserve honor (like Mordecai). But the Lord is the "rewarder of those who diligently seek Him" (Hebrews 11:6).

4. HAMAN HAD JUST ENTERED: Yet again we see the perfect sovereignty of God at work, for he caused Haman to enter the king's court at the exact moment He chose.

5. HAMAN IS THERE, STANDING IN THE COURT: God is never hindered by human intentions. People make choices between good and evil, and the Lord can use those choices to further His plans. The Lord was able to use even Haman's wicked scheme to further His purposes—though the wicked eventually find their own plans lashing back against themselves.

6. HAMAN THOUGHT IN HIS HEART: Ironically, Haman defined the honor to be given to Mordecai at his own expense. He thought public acclaim would be added to him in addition to the potential wealth he would gain from the Jewish plunder. Haman thought only of his own advancement at all times, even when he had done nothing to warrant it. Just as the Lord rewards the righteous, He also rewards wickedness with its own fruit in due season.

8. LET A ROYAL ROBE BE BROUGHT . . . ROYAL CREST PLACED ON ITS HEAD: This was an honor in which the recipient was treated as though he were the king himself. History affirms that horses were adorned with the royal crown.

9. PARADE HIM ON HORSEBACK THROUGH THE CITY SQUARE: To parade through the streets on a royal horse, wearing the king's own robes, would have told the people of the city that the honored man was to be obeyed with the same authority as the king. Of course, Haman's motivation for making these suggestions was based in greed, for he thought all these honors were coming his way. He would quickly be disappointed.

HAMAN'S DISAPPOINTMENT: To Haman's shock and amazement, the king commands him to honor his enemy, Mordecai, with the privileges Haman thought would be bestowed on he himself.

10. DO SO FOR MORDECAI THE JEW: The sudden and ironic reversal of fortune in this history is worthy of great literature—something that a writer like Shakespeare might have invented. But these events are true, not a work of

fiction. The Lord allowed Haman's perversity to define and engineer his own humiliation.

12. HAMAN HURRIED TO HIS HOUSE: Here is yet another interesting contrast between these two antagonists. After Haman had been honored and elevated, he went home and threw a party to celebrate, boasting grossly before family and friends about his great accomplishments. However, after Mordecai was honored and elevated, he went back to work. He had earned his preferment in contrast to Haman, yet he demonstrated the quality of his character by not letting it go to his head. He continued to diligently serve the king as he had always done.

MOURNING AND WITH HIS HEAD COVERED: What a difference a day makes! Haman's imagined honors had quickly turned to his unimaginable humiliation, and he had now inherited Mordecai's distress. He covered his head as an extreme sign of shame.

13. YOU HAVE BEGUN TO FALL: Neither divine prophecy (see Exodus 17:14) nor biblical history (see 1 Samuel 15:8–9) stood in Haman's favor. Haman's entourage seemed to have some knowledge of this fact.

14. HASTENED TO BRING HAMAN TO THE BANQUET: Like a lamb led to slaughter, Haman was escorted off to receive his just due.

REVERSAL OF FORTUNES: Queen Esther holds another banquet for the king and Haman, and at this one she makes her request to save the Jews from annihilation.

7:1. WENT TO DINE WITH QUEEN ESTHER: This is the second banquet that Esther held for the king and Haman. For the third time, the king asked what it was she wanted.

3. LET MY LIFE BE GIVEN ME: This plea paralleled God's message through Moses to Pharaoh, "Let my people go," almost 1,000 years before (Exodus 7:16). The king did not know at this point that Esther was a Jew, but as we have noted, Haman had also carefully failed to mention who the people were that he intended to exterminate. The king had been unwise in giving Haman such carte blanche in his decree, but now the truth was coming to light.

4. WE HAVE BEEN SOLD: Esther referred back to Haman's huge bribe of silver. She finally revealed that she was a Jew, but more importantly she openly identified herself with the people of God. She was saying that if the

king chose to go forward with the extermination of the Jews, she was determined to share their fate.

THE ENEMY COULD NEVER COMPENSATE FOR THE KING'S LOSS: This suggests that Esther was appealing to the king's self-interest just as Haman had done, pointing out that the Jews would be worth more alive in the long run than Haman's huge bribe. Other Bibles translate this phrase somewhat differently, suggesting it would not have been worthwhile to bother the king with such a small matter as the enslavement of the Jews. Either way, Esther was making it clear to Ahasuerus that he was going to suffer loss from Haman's wicked scheme.

> HAMAN'S DOWNFALL: *In one sudden moment, the Lord turns Haman's wicked schemes away from the Jews and toward his own household.*

6. THIS WICKED HAMAN: Similar to the prophet Nathan's famous accusation against King David, "You are the man" (2 Samuel 12:7), Haman's honor had quickly turned to humiliation—and then to horror.

7. THE KING AROSE IN HIS WRATH: King Ahasuerus was suddenly confronted with the realization that again he had been persuaded by his courtiers to endanger his own queen. He had already sacrificed his marriage to Vashti at their advice, and now he stood to lose his beloved Esther as well. His wrath was undoubtedly doubled by the fact that Haman had persuaded him through deceit, betraying the great trust the king had freely bestowed on him.

THE PALACE GARDEN: Once again we see the Lord's sovereign hand guiding the smallest details in this remarkable series of events. The king stormed out of the room to regain his composure and think clearly about what to do in the situation. This absence gave Haman the chance to throw himself at the queen's feet—literally, as it turned out.

8. HAMAN HAD FALLEN ACROSS THE COUCH: Haman's sudden reversal of position—from the king's favorite to the king's enemy—disconcerted him, and he evidently lost his balance. His position on the queen's couch was enough to forfeit his life, for Persian law dictated that no man except chosen eunuchs could ever be alone with any woman of the king's household. When Ahasuerus returned, he interpreted Haman's plea as an act of violence against Esther rather than a plea for mercy.

THEY COVERED HAMAN'S FACE: In that moment, Haman's fate was sealed and the king's servants covered his face. In the ancient world, this indicated the person had been condemned to death. The idea was that the person's last view of this world would be of the judge who had pronounced his or her doom.

9. THE GALLOWS . . . HAMAN MADE FOR MORDECAI: The place Haman had prepared for Mordecai's execution towered above the city, which made it the obvious spot for Haman's death. Haman would have heard this third charge against him: not only had he manipulated the king and appeared to accost the queen, but he had also sought to execute a man the king had just honored for loyalty to the kingdom.

10. THEY HANGED HAMAN ON THE GALLOWS THAT HE HAD PREPARED FOR MORDECAI: Haman's treacherous plans backfired. This is the final result for anyone who attempts to defy God, and just as surely, all who obey God will enjoy His protection and sovereign guidance.

THE KING'S WRATH SUBSIDED: Haman's life had ended, yet the problem still remained as to how to reverse the order, as edicts from the king could not be undone. The solution was for the king to allow the Jews to take up arms—"to destroy, kill, and annihilate all the forces of any people or province that would assault them" (Esther 8:11). On the day that Haman had plotted to exterminate the Jews, the Jews themselves overpowered their enemies (see 9:1).

UNLEASHING THE TEXT

1) Why did Esther invite King Ahasuerus to a banquet instead of asking him outright to save her people? Why did she invite Haman to attend the banquet as well?

_____

_____

_____

_____

2) How did God use Haman's pride against him in this story? How did Haman's greed and desire for importance lead to Mordecai being honored like a king?

_____

_____

_____

3) What caused the king to leave the room in fury? What caused him to condemn Haman to death when he returned?

_____

_____

_____

4) What evidence do you see in these passages of God's sovereign control? How might you have viewed these events if you have been living through them at the time?

_____

_____

_____

REFLECTING ON THE TEXT

Do not forget God's commands. Mordecai's refusal to again bow before Haman might appear at first to be stubborn pride, but that was not typical of his character. He was devoted to the king's service and diligent in his work, and his refusal to bow was motivated by his commitment to the Word of God. The Lord had commanded His people not to forget the sins of the Amalekites and

His judgment against that nation (see Deuteronomy 25:19), and Mordecai was "remembering to remember."

Remembering God's Word requires a deliberate choice on our part, because forgetting His commands is an inherent part of our fallen nature. This is the reason the Lord stressed the importance of remembering His Word, commanding His people, "Only take heed to yourself, and diligently keep yourself, lest you forget the things your eyes have seen, and lest they depart from your heart all the days of your life. And teach them to your children and your grandchildren" (Deuteronomy 4:9). The Lord further warned His people that forgetting His Word would lead them to say in their hearts, "My power and the might of my hand have gained me this wealth" (8:17). This was the very sin that Haman committed.

God's commands to "take heed" and "diligently keep yourself" demonstrate that remembering His Word requires ongoing effort on our part. Taking heed involves paying attention to our actions and attitudes and constantly double-checking them against the Scriptures. Keeping ourselves diligently requires spending time each day in the Lord's presence, confessing sins and seeking His guidance. It is through such daily disciplines, coupled with the indwelling power of the Holy Spirit, that God's people remember to remember.

We are responsible for obedience, and God is responsible for what follows. Mordecai obeyed God's commands with diligence and was faithful to carry out his duties at the king's gate. In fact, nearly every time he is mentioned in Esther, he can be found at the gate. Dealing with secret plots against the king's life probably did not fall into his job description, yet he understood he had an obligation before the Lord to protect the king and reveal that plot. He obeyed God and left the consequences in His hands.

Mordecai also obeyed the Lord's Word by not bowing before Haman. He did so knowing that he was making a powerful enemy—yet he obeyed just the same. This attitude lay at the root of his admonition to Esther to approach the king on behalf of the Jews, even at risk of her own life. Esther, for her part, was also obedient to God's commands, and as a result, God was able to work through her to save the Jews living in exile.

It is important for us to remember that Mordecai and Esther did not know the end of the story as we do. They were actually living out the events, and there was no guarantee they would live to see the next day. Like Daniel's three friends in the fiery furnace, they were called on to obey the Lord without being told what consequences would follow. The same is true for us today: our job is to obey God's Word and trust Him for the outcome. The good news is that as God was faithful to His people in Esther's day, so He will prove faithful today.

Anger is often driven by lack of perspective. There is a rich irony in the fate of Haman, a man whose life was characterized by self-promotion and boasting. Haman had everything he could want, and nearly every person in the empire bowed before him. But he did not enjoy those blessings because he was so fixated on the one person who did *not* honor him. Haman's high self-regard made him blind to the notion that there might be others more worthy of honor than him. His suggestion to the king reflected the extent of his own greed and covetousness.

Haman was an immature person who refused to see his blessings because he was blinded by pride. To some degree, we might be able to see ourselves in Haman. We have been given everything important: our sins have been forgiven, we have access to God through prayer, and we get to go to heaven when we die. God has given us a mission to evangelize others and has given us His Spirit to accomplish that task. We have everything we could ever need, yet like Haman we often fail to see this and instead get angry over inconsequential events.

Believers can be angry at sin, and anger at people's rejection of the Lord is certainly understandable. But the reality is that we have no reason to be angry when we are slighted. We are not to love our own honor, but rather to care deeply about the honor of the Lord. Jesus, as our example, was filled with zeal for His Father's house (see John 2:17), but he turned the other cheek when He was wrongly attacked (see 19:2). Remembering the glories of God and our riches in Christ should keep us from being angry at the wrong things.

PERSONAL RESPONSE

5) If you had been in Mordecai's position, how would you have felt while being paraded around on the king's horse? How might it have affected your life in the long term?

_____

_____

_____

6) When have you been able to see some of God's reasons for times of hardship? When have you not been able to see His reasons? What role does faith play in the process?

_____

_____

_____

_____

7) What steps do you take on a regular basis to "remember to remember" God's Word? What other disciplines might be helpful?

_____

_____

_____

_____

8) How did God ultimately protect His people? How did He use all of the evil that had been intended against His followers for good?

_____

_____

_____

_____

PERSONAL RESPONSE

9) How do you respond to people who think they are superior to you? When do you tend to treat others that way? What will you do this week to learn to regard others as better than yourself?

_____

_____

_____

_____

10) What areas of your life at present require faith? What will you do this week to increase your faith in God's sovereignty over those areas?

_____

_____

_____

_____

12

REVIEWING KEY PRINCIPLES

DRAWING NEAR

As you look back at each of the studies of Daniel and Esther, what is the one thing that stood out to you the most? What is one new perspective you have learned?

_____

_____

_____

THE CONTEXT

During the course of these studies, we have witnessed God's people facing un-expected and dire circumstances. Daniel was forced to interpret a dream that was not even described to him. His friends Shadrach, Meshach, and Abed-Nego were thrown in a fiery furnace for refusing to bow to a false idol. Esther faced the prospect of death by entering the presence of the king without an invitation. At every turn, it seemed God's people faced the prospects of annihilation and destruction at the hands of political enemies.

In every case, however, God's people stood firm in their obedience to His Word, and each time God proved that He was both sovereign and faithful. God demonstrated to Daniel, Mordecai, and Esther—and to us—that He is absolutely in control over all human events and is never caught by surprise. He works all things together for good for those who fear Him (see Romans 8:28), and nothing can touch His people without His permission.

Here are a few of the major principles we have found during our study. There are many more we don't have room to reiterate, so take some time to review the earlier studies—or, better still, to meditate on the Scripture that we have covered. As you do, ask the Holy Spirit to give you wisdom and insight into God's Word. He will not refuse.

EXPLORING THE MEANING

The Lord may allow hardship, but He is still in control. The nations of Israel and Judah had persisted in idolatry and disobedience to God's commands, and the time came for God to send His discipline against them. The nation of Israel was carried into captivity by the Assyrians, and years later the people of Judah suffered the same fate at the hands of the Babylonians. The walls of Jerusalem were torn down, the temple was razed, and the people's homes were plundered and burned. Those who survived became prisoners of war and were carried away to a distant land—a land that neither feared God nor knew His Word.

Yet the Lord was still in control over all these circumstances, and He had not abandoned His people. He was sending a time of suffering to the Jews, but that hardship was intended for their purification and their strengthening, and it was all part of His plan. Furthermore, the Lord promised through His prophets that it would only be for a limited time. At the end of seventy years, God would call some of His people to return and rebuild Jerusalem.

Throughout the course of these studies, we saw that God is in complete control over all circumstances in the lives of His people—even during those times when life seems to be spiraling out of control. Just as He directed the steps of Daniel and his friends, He will do so in our lives as well. As Samuel's mother, Hannah, said, "The LORD kills and makes alive; He brings down to the grave and brings up. The LORD makes poor and makes rich; He brings low and lifts up. He raises the poor from the dust and lifts the beggar from the ash heap, to set them among princes and make them inherit the throne of glory. For the pillars of the earth are the LORD's, and He has set the world upon them. He will guard the feet of His saints" (1 Samuel 2:6–9).

Man's wrath does not produce God's righteousness. It would appear that Nebuchadnezzar's temper was modeled after his furnaces: fiery! When his magicians asked what his dream was before offering an interpretation, he roared, "If you do not make known the dream to me, and its interpretation, you shall be cut in pieces, and your houses shall be made an ash heap" (Daniel 2:5). His rage flared up instantly when his will was thwarted, and his punishments were extreme. Even after he realized that Daniel's friends served Almighty God, he resorted to his old threat of cutting into pieces any who spoke ill of God, making their houses as ash heaps.

The truth is that Nebuchadnezzar's anger was a natural consequence of his pride, not a righteous indignation against defiance or unlawful behavior. It was his pride that led him to create the golden image and command his nation to worship it, and that pride had been offended when Daniel's friends refused to comply. His subsequent anger clouded his judgment, and he ended up defying the God of creation. If the king had humbled himself and cooled his anger, he might have recognized that the men's testimony was true and that his image was nothing more than a false god.

James warned his readers of the deadly trap of human wrath: "So then, my beloved brethren, let every man be swift to hear, slow to speak, slow to wrath; for the wrath of man does not produce the righteousness of God" (James 1:19–20). The Lord had raised Daniel's friends as a witness to the king, in order to offer him the chance to hear the truth concerning his idolatrous practices, but the king had refused to listen. Instead, he was quick to speak and quick to indulge his wrath, and as a result he quickly fell into deadly error. When anger flares up, take time to listen and pray. Quick speech can result in negative long-term consequences.

Pride debases a man, but humility lifts him up. The world looked at King Nebuchadnezzar and saw a man who had enjoyed success in every venture—a man who had reached the pinnacle of human achievement. Then one day he went insane. His subjects watched aghast as he foraged through his royal garden, shuffling about on hands and knees and eating grass like a cow. They watched as his hair and nails grew filthy and unkempt and the rain and dew fell unheeded on his skin. They must have wondered how such a great man could be so suddenly debased.

When God looked on Nebuchadnezzar, He did not see the pinnacle of humanity but a man who had degraded his soul through pride and vanity. It was not a coincidence that the Lord chose to have the king go about on all fours, for in this way God permitted the true nature of Nebuchadnezzar's pride to become evident to himself and the people around him. Pride is the sin of elevating oneself to equality with God, and the paradoxical result is that it actually moves one *away* from God rather than toward Him. Human beings are made in the image of God, so any move away from God is also a move away from our intended design—a move that makes us more like the beasts of the field.

Solomon wrote, "The fear of the LORD is to hate evil; pride and arrogance and the evil way and the perverse mouth I [the Lord] hate" (Proverbs 8:13). "When pride comes, then comes shame; but with the humble is wisdom" (11:2). "Pride goes before destruction, and a haughty spirit before a fall" (16:18). Nebuchadnezzar had to learn the lesson that "a man's pride will bring him low, but the humble in spirit will retain honor" (29:23).

God gives His people the words to speak at the right time. As we have seen throughout this study, Daniel found himself in difficult situations on numerous occasions. He was called before several kings to interpret messages from God that no one else in the kingdom could comprehend—and at times his life was on the line. The Lord had given him the gift of interpreting dreams and prophecies, and Daniel made it abundantly clear that the messages were from the Lord and that they did not come through his own strength, wisdom, or abilities. God was faithful in each instance to give Daniel the words he was to speak.

It is important to recognize, however, that Daniel did not know what he would say until the time came for him to speak. Just as he had not known the content of Nebuchadnezzar's dream until the Lord revealed it to him, he did not know what words were written on the wall in Belshazzar's banquet hall until he arrived there. We can easily imagine how unnerving it must have been for him to have no idea what to say to a king who demanded an interpretation—especially given that all the other wise men had failed. Yet this was precisely what the Lord called His servant to do. This forced Daniel to trust in God's faithfulness and sovereignty and made it clear to the king and his court that the words were from Him.

Peter urged his readers to "always be ready to give a defense to everyone who asks you a reason for the hope that is in you" (1 Peter 3:15). Christians should always be prepared to give a clear account of their testimony to others. Yet Jesus also warned His disciples that they would sometimes "be brought before governors and kings" to give testimony to the gospel. At such times, the Lord said, "Do not worry about how or what you should speak. For it will be given to you in that hour what you should speak; for it is not you who speak, but the Spirit of your Father who speaks in you" (Matthew 10:18–20). This is not an excuse for a haphazard testimony but rather a comfort during persecution. Just as God was faithful to give Daniel the right words, He will do the same for us. We can have confidence that God will enable us to be a faithful witness no matter the situation in which we find ourselves.

God's people should live above reproach. The events of Daniel 6 present a profound statement of Daniel's godly character. His political enemies were motivated by base envy and were jealous of the favor the king showed to Daniel. Those enemies were the most powerful men in the kingdom, and they set all their power and resources on finding something that Daniel had done wrong. They wanted to uncover some shortcoming, failure, or character flaw with which to spoil his reputation—but they could find nothing!

Most people would cringe if they knew an enemy was trying to discover something they had done wrong. Yet that is exactly what is happening for every believer every day of the year! The enemy of our souls is the accuser of all believers, and he works diligently, day and night, to bring accusations of sin against all who place their faith in Jesus Christ (see Revelation 12:10). The blood of Christ permanently silences the devil's accusations, for through His sacrifice we are found blameless before God. However, this does not give believers the license to indulge in sin. Quite the opposite, in fact.

The Bible calls us to live lives that are above reproach so the enemy cannot find a foothold or a source of accusation against us. As Paul wrote, "Do all things without complaining and disputing, that you may become blameless and harmless, children of God without fault in the midst of a crooked and perverse generation, among whom you shine as lights in the world" (Philippians 2:14–15). Paul also instructed Titus on the qualities required of elders and deacons, but those qualities should be the goal for every believer: "For a bishop must be blameless, as a steward of God, not self-willed, not quick-tempered, not given to wine, not violent, not greedy for money, but hospitable, a lover of what is good, sober-minded, just, holy, self-controlled, holding fast the faithful word as he has been taught" (Titus 1:7–9). When our lives are above reproach, we shine like beacons in a world of darkness.

Provoking others leads to wrath. Queen Vashti did have legitimate reason for resenting the king's summons to his banquet. She probably felt that she was being used as a political tool or a prized possession. Furthermore, being paraded in front of a room of leering men would be degrading and offensive to any woman—and Vashti was the queen! Rather than being highly concerned with his wife's welfare and virtue, the king felt no qualms about exposing her to the eyes of strangers. No wonder the queen was not pleased with the command!

Nevertheless, the queen's response was not wise. Her husband's command certainly risked humiliating her, but that did not excuse her for publicly humiliating him in return. Furthermore, Ahasuerus was the king, which means that Vashti's defiant response was against a God-ordained authority. Proverbs rightly warns, "The wrath of a king is like the roaring of a lion; whoever provokes him to anger sins against his own life. It is honorable for a man to stop striving, since any fool can start a quarrel" (20:2–3).

Daniel and his friends demonstrated this principle when they first arrived in Babylon by gently offering an alternative to the king's command concerning forbidden foods. They were able to avoid disobeying God's commands while also not provoking the king to wrath. Paul pointed out that the root of provocation is pride—the idea that our desires are more important than someone else's. He offered a better approach: "But the fruit of the Spirit is love, joy, peace, longsuffering, kindness, goodness, faithfulness, gentleness, self-control. Against such there is no law. And those who are Christ's have crucified the flesh with its passions and desires. If we live in the Spirit, let us also walk in the Spirit. Let us not become conceited, provoking one another, envying one another" (Galatians 5:22–26).

God puts us where He wants us for His specific purposes. Joseph had once rocketed from a prison pit to the throne of Egypt, the most powerful nation in the world at the time. Daniel had gone from being a prisoner of war to being the most trusted counselor of the Babylonians, another powerful nation of its day. In the same manner, we see a young Jewish woman named Esther suddenly whisked from complete obscurity to become queen of the world's most powerful empire. It is easy, in retrospect, to see God's sovereign hand in such instances because they are so dramatic and miraculous.

Yet the same principle is always at work in the mundane day-to-day realities of our lives. Esther was indeed whisked to the throne, but before that could happen, she had to endure being wrenched from her home and family and married without having her own inclinations considered. Year after year, Mordecai worked a steady job that probably did not seem dramatic or miraculous—yet the Lord placed him exactly where he needed to be. Even Daniel had to endure a lengthy period of uncertainty and danger before he saw God's miraculous blessings.

The fact is that before God could reveal His miraculous plans for these people, they were required for a period of time to be faithful to some less-dramatic occupation. The same principle holds true for us: God has placed us exactly where He wants us to be in order to work out a bigger plan in our lives and in the lives of others. Esther and Mordecai could not see what God intended to do through them, and neither can we. Our job is to work diligently and faithfully wherever the Lord has placed us, and He will take care of the future.

We are responsible for obedience, and God is responsible for what follows. Mordecai obeyed God's commands with diligence and was faithful to carry out his duties at the king's gate. In fact, nearly every time he is mentioned in Esther, he can be found at the gate. Dealing with secret plots against the king's life probably did not fall into his basic job description, yet he understood he had an obligation before the Lord to protect the king and reveal that plot. He obeyed God and left the consequences in His hands.

Mordecai also obeyed the Lord's Word by not bowing before Haman. He did so knowing that he was making a powerful enemy—yet he obeyed just the same. This attitude lay at the root of his admonition to Esther to approach the king on behalf of the Jews, even at risk of her own life. Esther, for her part, was also obedient to God's commands, and as result God was able to work through her to save the Jews living in exile.

It is important for us to remember that Mordecai and Esther did not know the end of the story as we do. They were actually living out the events, and there was no guarantee they would live to see tomorrow. Like Daniel's three friends in the fiery furnace, they were called on to obey the Lord without being told what consequences would follow. The same is true for us today: our job is to obey God's Word and trust Him for the outcome. The good news is that He has not changed since Esther's day. As He was faithful to His people then, so He will prove faithful today and tomorrow.

Unleashing the Text

1) Which of the concepts or principles in this study have you found to be the most encouraging? Why?

_____

_____

_____

_____

2) Which of the concepts or principles have you found most challenging? Why?

_____

_____

_____

_____

3) What aspects of "walking with God" are you already doing in your life? Which areas need strengthening?

_____

_____

_____

_____

4) To which of the characters that we've studied have you been able to relate? How might you emulate that person in your own life?

_____

_____

_____

_____

PERSONAL RESPONSE

5) Have you taken a definite stand for Jesus Christ? Have you accepted His free gift of salvation? If not, what is preventing you from doing so?

_____

_____

_____

6) In what areas of your life have you been convicted during this study? What exact things will you do to address these convictions? Be specific.

_____

_____

_____

_____

7) What have you learned about the character of God during this study? How has this insight affected your worship and prayer life?

_____

_____

_____

_____

8) What are some specific things you want to see God do in your life in the coming month? What are some things you intend to change in your own life during that time? (Return to this list in one month and hold yourself accountable to fulfill these things.)

_____

_____

_____

_____

If you would like to continue in your study of the Old Testament, read the next title in this series: _Ezra & Nehemiah: Israel Returns from Exile._

ALSO AVAILABLE

In this study, John MacArthur guides readers through an in-depth look at the historical period beginning with God's calling of Moses, continuing through the giving of the Ten Commandments, and concluding with the Israelites' preparations to enter the Promised Land. This study includes close-up examinations of Aaron, Caleb, Joshua, Balaam and Balak, as well as careful considerations of doctrinal themes such as "Complaints and Rebellion" and "Following God's Law."

The MacArthur Bible Studies provide intriguing examinations of the whole of Scripture. Each guide incorporates extensive commentary, detailed observations on overriding themes, and probing questions to help you study the Word of God with guidance from John MacArthur.

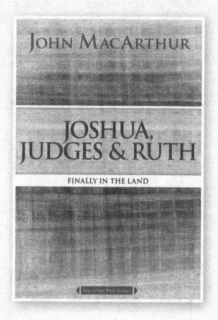

In this study, John MacArthur guides readers through an in-depth look at the Israelites' conquest of the Promised Land, beginning with the miraculous parting of the Jordan River, continuing through the victories and setbacks as the people settled into Canaan, and concluding with the time of the judges. Studies include close-up examinations of Rahab, Ruth, and Samson, as well as careful considerations of doctrinal themes such as "The Sin of Achan" and the role of "The Kinsman Redeemer."

The MacArthur Bible Studies provide intriguing examinations of the whole of Scripture. Each guide incorporates extensive commentary, detailed observations on overriding themes, and probing questions to help you study the Word of God with guidance from John MacArthur.

9780718034719-A

ALSO AVAILABLE

In this study, John MacArthur guides readers through an in-depth look at this historical period beginning with the miraculous birth of Samuel, continuing through Saul's crowning as Israel's first king, and concluding with his tragic death. Studies include close-up examinations of Hannah, Eli, Saul, David, and Jonathan, as well as careful considerations of doctrinal themes such as "Slaying a Giant" and "Respecting God's Anointed."

The MacArthur Bible Studies provide intriguing examinations of the whole of Scripture. Each guide incorporates extensive commentary, detailed observations on overriding themes, and probing questions to help you study the Word of God with guidance from John MacArthur.

ALSO AVAILABLE

In this study, John MacArthur guides readers through an in-depth look at the historical period beginning with David's struggle to establish his throne, continuing through his sin and repentance, and concluding with the tragic rebellion of his son Absalom. Studies include close-up examinations of Joab, Amnon, Tamar, Absalom, and others, as well as careful considerations of doctrinal themes such as "Obedience and Blessing" and being a "Man After God's Own Heart."

The MacArthur Bible Studies provide intriguing examinations of the whole of Scripture. Each guide incorporates extensive commentary, detailed observations on overriding themes, and probing questions to help you study the Word of God with guidance from John MacArthur.